PENNSYLVANIA-READING SEASHORE LINES
In Color

By John P. Stroup

Copyright © 1996
Morning Sun Books, Inc.

Published by
Morning Sun Books, Inc.
11 Sussex Court
Edison, N.J. 08820

Library of Congress Catalog Card Number: 96-075351
Typesetting and layout by R.B. George, Jr., with assistance from
John P. Stroup and Robert J. Yanosey

First Printing
ISBN 1-878887-57-2

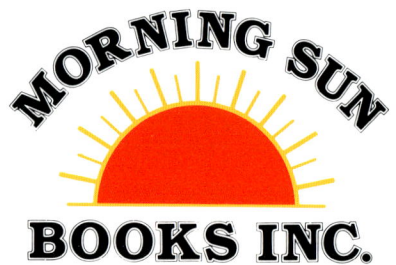

DEDICATION

To the memory of my mother and dad, Helen and Willard Stroup, who encouraged and praised my photography, even when it meant sitting through innumerable slide shows of nothing but trains.

ACKNOWLEDGEMENTS

The photographic contributions of Ron Baile, Will Coxey, Joe Grella, Al Holtz, Ed Kelsey, Frank Kozempel, Bob Long, Dick Short, Karl Then, and Bill and Steve Tilden are gratefully appreciated. Their willingness to share the results of their trackside endeavors have greatly enriched the scope of photographic coverage presented in this book. The encouragement, patience and understanding of family and friends was truly appreciated, without which an idea would never have become a book. A special thanks to Will Coxey is due, as his extensive knowledge of the PRSL contributed greatly to bringing an additional perspective to this work. He also generously helped with proofreading and editing the text, which was a lengthy task. And of course, thanks to Bob Yanosey of Morning Sun Books for his suggestions and faith in publishing a work about an admittedly "minor" railroad. Also material from his collection as well as from Will Coxey has greatly enhanced the finished work.

For more detailed further historical information, the following sources are recommended:

Several books about southern New Jersey railroading by the West Jersey Chapter, National Railway Historical Society, P.O. Box 647, Palmyra, NJ 08065; and the book **BY RAIL TO THE BOARDWALK** by Richard M. Gladulich, published by Trans-Anglo Books, P.O. Box 6444, Glendale, CA 91205.

The station pages and freight schedules herein are from the June 19, 1960, PRSL Employee Timetable, and maps by the author reflect that period.

PENNSYLVANIA-READING
SEASHORE LINES

The Pennsylvania-Reading Seashore Lines was a small railroad with a big following. For those outside of the area, the PRSL appeared to many to be "just another Pennsy branch," and was quickly dismissed from thought. But what a mistake, for here was high speed running performed by finely-tuned motive power from both the PRR and Reading as well as the PRSL itself. Here also were through trains from numerous points on the Pennsy, as well as through cars from all over the country.

While the topography is not hilly, a ride to the southern New Jersey coast did provide fine vistas of well-kept small towns, rich farmlands, pine forests, salt marshes and bays that gradually gave way to the great Atlantic Ocean. While the lines to the shore were primarily passenger routes, the inland lines tapped great agricultural and industrial areas. Closer to Camden, commuters were accommodated.

The objective of the early companies in the construction of the rail lines to the coastal areas was to develop a brisk passenger trade by encouraging the creation of the resorts themselves. The concept was generally quite successful. In fact, to many points a rival railroad was hurriedly laid down, especially after the Pennsylvania Railroad and Reading System acquired the two competing lines to Atlantic City in the 1880s.

Both companies reached further south to serve Ocean City, Wildwood and Cape May as well as numerous other coastal communities. They also saw the potential of traffic in agriculture and light manufacturing further to the west as they bought or constructed trackage throughout the remainder of southern New Jersey. As the turn of the century approached, the railroads of the nation had a virtual monopoly in land transport of people and goods, and that scenario was also played out in southern New Jersey.

On the Atlantic City main lines, competition reigned by the 1890s as the PRR and RDG tried to outdo the other; eventually the only difference that could be offered was the length of the journey to the shore. Constantly vying for the public's attention, the race continued with larger and faster motive power into the 1920s.

The Pennsylvania Railroad gained an important edge when its all-rail route from Philadelphia via the Delair Bridge was completed in 1897. No longer did Philadelphians and travelers from other areas need to go across town to the west bank of the Delaware River and ride a ferryboat to Camden before finally boarding their train. Of course, this circuitous route took longer and was of no use for downtown commuters heading for Millville or Collingswood, for example. So a large demand continued for the Camden ferry services.

Although southern New Jersey development increased as the new century progressed, changes were also occurring that would bring about the need for the elimination of duplicate rail services. The roots of the consolidation began in the 1920s as roads were improved and the first highway bridge between Philadelphia and Camden was built. What had been a captive market soon saw the challenges of busses and trucks as the highway network grew and became paved. The Reading's Atlantic City Railroad and the Pennsy's West Jersey and Seashore were now faced with outside threats to their own long-standing competition. The market was now being divided not only between them, but with bus companies and more importantly, private automobiles. Recognizing that the trend of declining traffic and growing losses was irreversible, a merger was jointly proposed by the two carriers. After many hearings with input from state, county and local authorities, agreement was finally reached and the new jointly-owned company established effective June 25, 1933. Due to the more extensive mileage of the West Jersey and Seashore, the PRR was given two-thirds interest in the line with the Reading the remainder.

During the remaining years of the 1930s, trackage removal and other cost reduction measures took place. However, as World War II gained momentum and involved the United States, the railroads, including the PRSL, were faced with great demands, as both passenger and freight business was booming. Stored equipment was pressed into service in order to accommodate the expanded demand for rail service, as new additions were almost impossible to obtain.

When the war was over, a post-war boom for the PRSL soon turned into another bust, as the customer's needs and desires were fulfilled by other means. The trend to highway travel resumed at a much greater pace than ever before. As traffic declined, the PRSL effected cost-saving efforts: included were discontinuance of the Camden-Millville electric MU service in 1949, and a general reduction in all passenger service which left the Penns Grove, Salem, Bridgeton and Newfield Branches freight-only by 1952, the year PRR Delaware River ferry service ceased. Further economies were produced as diesels and RDCs began to arrive, working side by side with PRR and Reading steam.

Meanwhile another decline was occurring in southern New Jersey: that of Atlantic City. When the original railroad to the shore was being completed in 1853, there still was no given name for the uninhabited destination of the line. The civil engineer had placed the name **ATLANTIC CITY** on the route map, and being duly impressed, the board of directors embraced the name. So, from the beginning, Atlantic City and the railroad grew together. For about one hundred years the two entities prospered as "America's Playground" became known for the "Steel Pier," various conventions, "Miss America," a multitude of fine hotels, seafood, salt water taffy and the boardwalk. But as the post-war era brought about new prosperity for many Americans, it also brought about the decline of Atlantic City. No longer was it the place of choice for Philadelphians and New Yorkers. The city and the railroad were now declining together. Service reductions continued to occur during the 1950s, and by the spring of 1961 the schedule had been reduced to four Philadelphia weekday round trips with three on the weekends. Camden-Atlantic City service consisted of two weekday-only round trips.

Fortunately for the railroad, freight traffic was growing because of new heavy industries including chemical and fiberglass plants together with distribution warehouses located in several new industrial parks in Camden and Gloucester Counties. Also an electric utility converted one generating plant from oil to coal and built a new large facility. This traffic increase contributed to a chronic shortage of motive power which would plague the railroad for much of its remaining years.

Meanwhile, the Pennsylvania Railroad, through merger with the New York Central, had become the Penn Central, which assumed the two-thirds interest in the PRSL effective February 1, 1968. During the next few years, the fortunes of most of the Northeastern railroads continued to erode and one by one they went bankrupt, including the Penn Central and the Reading. The PRSL was plunged into this economic whirlpool which led to it being included in Conrail in 1976; after nearly forty-three years, what was once a unique and intriguing railroad was absorbed into a huge corporation.

The following pages present a glimpse of primarily the last two decades of this fascinating railroad. During the first seven years of the 1950s, diesel power replaced steam and the passenger trains became shorter and less frequent. Next, the original diesels gave way to the "second generation," and finally the railroad itself ceased to exist. Photos can convey only one facet of change; but they can help stir memories for those who personally witnessed southern New Jersey's own railroad. They can also show future generations what transpired before their footprints mingled with those of their ancestors, trackside in southern New Jersey.

The map above is from a 1937 brochure expounding the many benefits of traveling to the seashore upon the Pennsylvania-Reading Seashore Lines. It was mainly directed toward fishermen, and was replete with quotes from "Barnacle Bill." *(Robert J. Yanosey Collection)*

PHILADELPHIA

Philadelphia, "The City of Brotherly Love," long the nation's third largest city until the post-war era reduced that rating, was the headquarters of both the Pennsylvania Railroad and the Reading Company. Philadelphia overshadowed southern New Jersey's commerce and most railroads pointed in its direction. In addition to its own millions who were employed within the city, thousands more commuted there from suburbs in Pennsylvania as well as New Jersey, as did shoppers, students, and cultural and historical devotees.

Philadelphians were the primary patrons of the railroads to the New Jersey shore. With its millions of eager vacationers dreaming of that getaway from the city's heat and noise in the summer, it's little wonder that the trains usually were filled to capacity and at times multiple sections were needed in addition to the many scheduled trains during the three month "season." With the formation of the Pennsylvania-Reading Seashore Lines, the new railroad continued to utilize the PRR's Philadelphia facilities.

The seashore trains originated at Broad Street Station in downtown Philadelphia until that facility was closed in 1952. Then 30th Street Station became the major Philadelphia terminal, with the North Philadelphia stop continuing primarily as a station to make connections, particularly to and from The "Mainline."

(Above) A train bound for the Atlantic City race track is seen from North 33rd Street, just east of Fairmount Park. On this early fall day of September 23, 1967, the train is powered by the 6012 and 6016. *(William M. Tilden)*

Completed in 1896, the Delair Bridge served a two-fold purpose. It provided direct access to Pavonia Yard in Camden for the burgeoning southern New Jersey freight traffic, eliminating a slow and costly car float transfer. It also facilitated through passenger service for the southern New Jersey shore resorts after the connecting line reached Haddonfield in 1897. At the west end of the Bridge Branch at Frankford Junction in northeastern Philadelphia, the Pennsy constructed **SHORE** tower. What more appropriate name could have been chosen? The tower controlled the junction of the double-track seashore route with the six track mainline. To the east, just beyond the station platform, was an engine servicing facility and small yard which the Pennsy utilized to serve industries in the area. Most Camden freight trains made set-offs and pick-ups here, even into the Conrail era.

(Above) Strictly by coincidence, all three photos on these pages have the 6016 for power. It's 11:30 a.m. on September 29, 1962, and Train #1011 is passing the original (and only) 1896 **SHORE** tower, just east of the Frankford Elevated transit line spanning the railroad. In a moment the train will make its Frankford Junction station stop.

(Below) This is Train #1022, the 3 p.m. departure from Atlantic City, easing to a stop at the station on February 17, 1968. Soon it will cross over two main line tracks to Track #3 in preparation for a stop at North Philadelphia and then on to complete its journey at 30th Street. Note the huge textile mills, long a local landmark along the New York-Philadelphia main line, the busiest piece of railroad in the nation. *(Both – John P. Stroup)*

After crossing the bridge over the wide Delaware River, the traveler reaches New Jersey, and is greeted by another very appropriately named tower, **JERSEY**, located in the Delair section of Pennsauken Township. Here the Camden-bound freights diverged on to a connecting track behind the tower to reach the Bordentown Branch and Pavonia Yard about two miles to the southwest. Also utilizing the Bordentown Branch, but in the opposite direction, were the direct New York-Atlantic City trains which operated over the Bridge Branch between **DIVIDE** interlocking, just south of **JERSEY**, and Haddonfield. **JERSEY** tower was built in 1937 when four small wooden towers were replaced.

(Above) In a panoramic view of this area, Train #1001, once again behind the 6016, accelerates southward past the switch at **DIVIDE** on this warm October 20, 1966. This train was the first trip of the day to Atlantic City, having departed 30th Street Station at 8:40 a.m. Until 1961 this train bore the name SEA BREEZE, the last named train between Philadelphia or Camden and the shore.
(William M. Tilden)

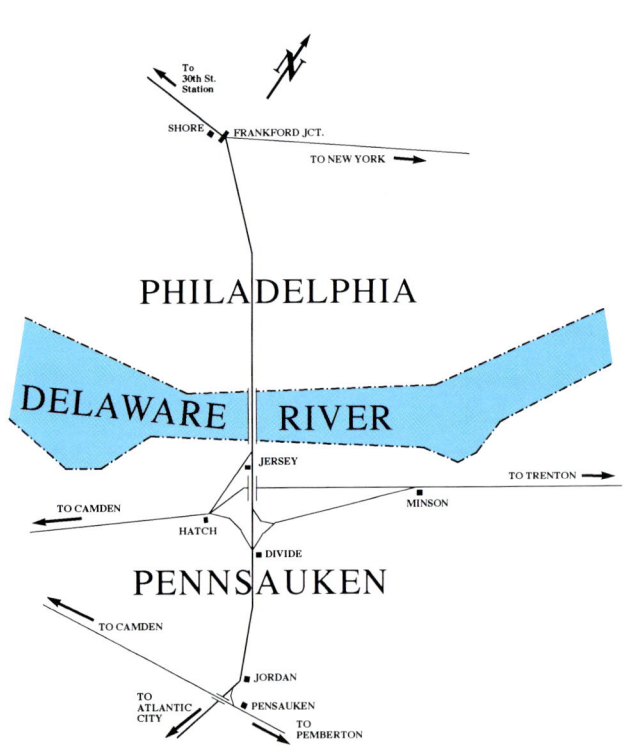

In addition to the usual duties associated with block operators, the **JERSEY** operator was also responsible for the safe opening of the Delair Bridge. Before the bridge tender could raise the vertical-lift span (a swing span prior to March 1960), the operator at **JERSEY** first had to set all home signals to "stop" and lower the smash boards.

(Top) Almost off the bridge, at about 6:45 p.m. on an evening in April 1966, Train #1033, the last Atlantic City train of the day, with the 6013 as power, shows clearly how massive this structure is. *(Steven W. Tilden)*

(Center) In this scene on April 11, 1966, Train #1001 passes **JERSEY**, operating with RDCs M406 and M411. This was during the first year of Budd Car use to Philadelphia, which was made possible by the discontinuance of most Camden service due to construction of the Patco Lindenwold High-Speed Line. This change came at a good time as there was a diminishing number of servicable P-70 coaches and a need for more diesels to handle growing freight business. *(John P. Stroup)*

(Bottom) Just south of the tower, the double-track Bridge Branch crosses the formerly double-tracked Bordentown Branch. Here is northbound Train #1022 being hustled toward Philadelphia by engine #6014 on August 7, 1965. As the PRSL roster of various types of passenger equipment shrunk, the carrier was forced to utilize PRR cars, eventually even coaches. Trains 1011 and 1022 were the last to be assigned a baggage car and this ended in November 1966. *(John P. Stroup)*

At **DIVIDE** interlocking, the Morris Branch conveyed New York trains east one mile to a connection with the Bordentown Branch at another **JERSEY**-controlled remote interlocking, **MINSON**. On Sunday May 23, 1943, New York-bound Train #1080 derailed upon entering the south leg of the wye at **DIVIDE** due to excessive speed, resulting in the death of twelve passengers and two crewmen. The power was K4s #3806, seen years later at Winslow on page 43.

(Above and below) Sister K4s #1120 powers Train #1072 past the very spot of #1080's wreck. The whistle is blowing for the Derousse Avenue crossing on this clear April 3, 1954. No. 1120 was one of four class K4s 4-6-2 Pacific-type locomotives which had semi-streamlined shrouding applied in 1940. Primarily for use on the steam-powered segment of THE BROADWAY LIMITED between Harrisburg and Chicago, these engines had the shrouding removed in later years to reduce maintenance costs and servicing time. *(Both – Frank C. Kozempel)*

The third remote interlocking, in addition to **DIVIDE** and **MINSON**, was **HATCH**, located at the west end of the Fish House Branch that provided the link to Pavonia Yard via the Bordentown Branch. In 1966 a connection was built between **HATCH** and **DIVIDE** to provide a new route for the Camden-Atlantic City freight, CA-289. This was one of the many changes necessitated by the construction of the Patco Lindenwold High-Speed Line, which completely usurped the PRSL right-of-way between Camden and Haddonfield. Thus for the first time, through scheduled freight service was seen along the PRR's Bridge Branch. This procedure lasted only until 1968, when the train was rerouted via the Clementon Branch to Winslow, and a reverse move made to deliver any cars destined between there and Woodcrest. Another crew handled business between Atlantic City and Winslow.

(Above) CA-289 works hard up the grade of the new connection behind engine #6000 on August 24, 1966. This roadswitcher is the first of thirty-four Baldwin locomotives that were obtained over a six year period. The first six locomotives were of model DRS 4-4-1500, which had been introduced in 1947. As it turned out, the PRSL units would be the last of a total of only thirty-five of this model produced. In 1950, a new model AS-16 was introduced by BLH, containing several refinements in addition to an increase of one hundred horsepower.

(Below) It's New Year's Eve, 1967, and a storm is raging as the 6016 brings Train #1022 northward past the signals at **DIVIDE**. In one more month this piece of railroad would become part of Penn Central, formed in an attempt to stabilize the eroding financial strength of the Pennsylvania Railroad and long-time rival New York Central. Unfortunately, stormy times were ahead for secondary lines such as the Bridge Branch when deferred maintenance became the norm. *(Both-Steven W. Tilden)*

Named for the nearby Jordantown section of Pennsauken Township, this block station is two miles south of **JERSEY** at Park Avenue. It provided shelter for block operators that were called to duty whenever a troop train was run to the huge Army training base of Fort Dix. Just south of the road crossing was the connecting track which led to the PRR's Pemberton Branch, and on to Fort Dix.

(Above) PRSL Train #1018 has just passed **JORDAN** on October 4, 1958, with PRR class AFP-20 (Alco PA-1) #5752 as power. This was during the time that all PRSL road power was being equippped with automatic train stop as mandated by the State of New Jersey following the tragic Newark Bay wreck on the Jersey Central the month before. During the next few years it was only in the summer months that Alco PAs and EMD E-7s were loaned to the PRSL to handle their seasonal requirements. The Alcos were only around once more in 1959 and thereafter the E-7s took over in 1960 and each summer through 1964.

(Below) Train #1001 rolls by behind the 6015 on May 23, 1965. The short consist was becoming quite common due to declining patronage, even on the mid-summer runs. *(Above - Frank C. Kozempel, below - Steven W. Tilden)*

(Right) This is Army MAIN 1025, otherwise known as Passenger Extra PRSL 6014 South, crossing over to the connecting track en route to Fort Dix with 265 new recruits. The train was made up with PRSL 6014 and 6026 on the point, followed by six Pullmans, PRR diners 4510 and 4485, and seven more Pullmans - fifteen cars in all. Strictly a PRR operation, it never-the-less was using PRSL diesels which were available on this Sunday July 1, 1962. These units took over from the road power, probably a GG-1 motor, in Philadelphia. Engineman Fred Philbrook and conductor Norm Hagaman, who normally worked the PRR Pemberton Branch's passenger train, were in charge. Charlie Howell, the block operator this day at **JORDAN**, was usually the day trick man at **JERSEY**.

(Below) Wildwood Train #1053 with RDCs M411 and M413 passes by on July 23, 1966. The PRSL had begun applying these safety stripes on their RDCs and the practice was picked up by the Reading when the PRSL Budds began to be rebuilt at their Reading, PA shops. The stripes would continue into the NJ Transit/SEPTA era on the former RDG Budd cars, and eventually show up throughout the U.S. as the RDCs were sold to museums and short line operators. *(Both -John P. Stroup)*

WEST JERSEY & SEASHORE RAILROAD.

Pass—S. B. Richards 1903

Account of

Philadelphia BETWEEN AND Atlantic City

Until December 31st 1903,

Unless otherwise ordered.

D W Lowe
Superintendent.

2

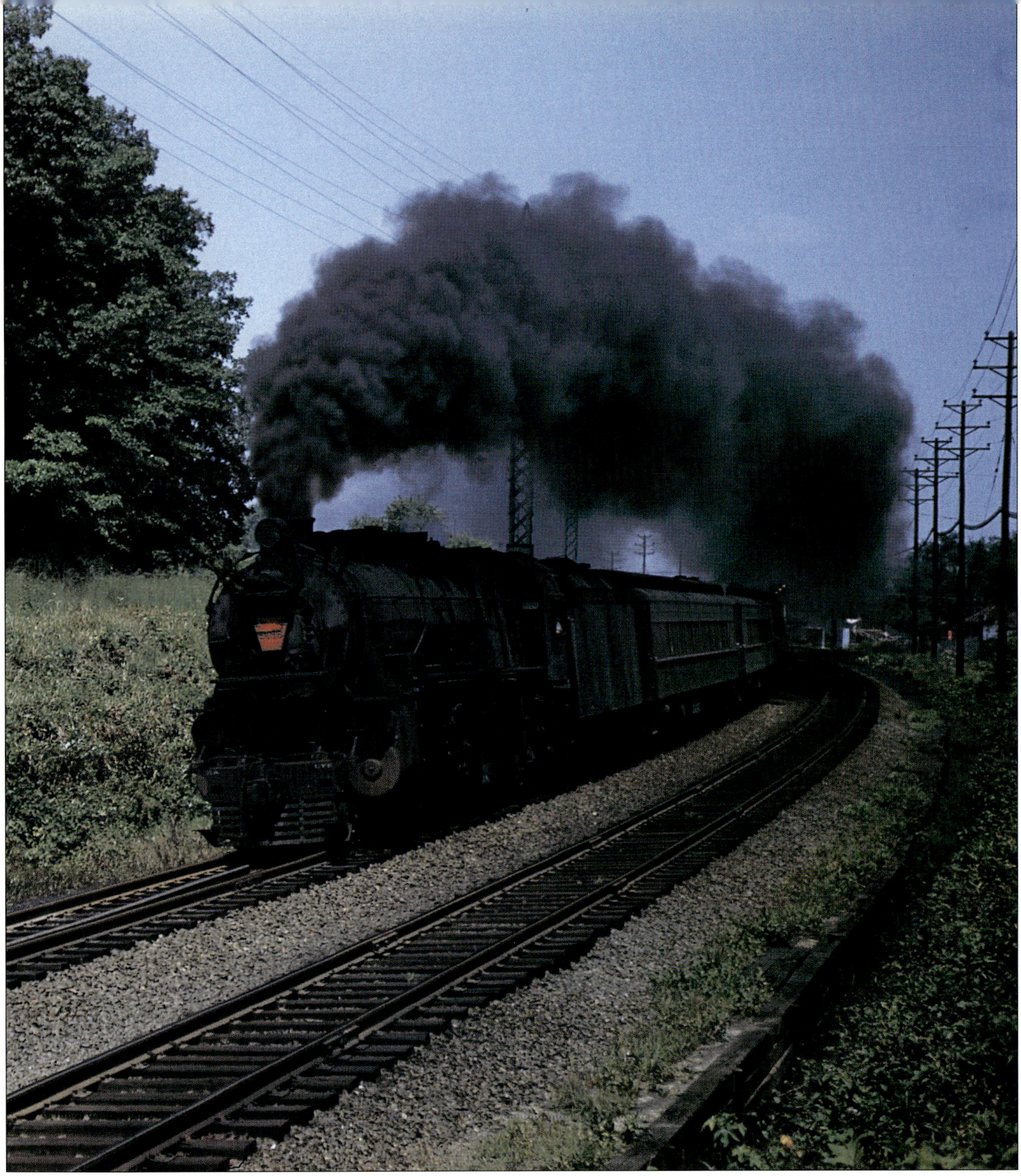

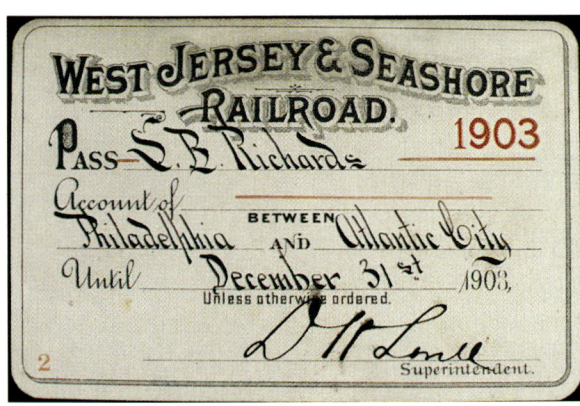

(Left) Passes such as this were issued over the years to employees, politicians and influential business people. During the 1960s it was alleged that there were more pass riders than paying passengers on the PRSL's continually money-losing trains. *(William J. Coxey Collection)*

These 1954 scenes at **JORDAN** show the magnificent K4s in its glory. Old – yes, but tired – No!

(Opposite page) On August 14, a nine-car Atlantic City race train is led by the 5495. Only eight K4s were produced in 1928 (#5492 - 5499) and they turned out to be the very last of this class.

(Above) On July 3, Train #1057 has fourteen cars behind the 1927-built 5414 as it heads to Wildwood.

(Below) #1059 roars by on August 14 with the 3674 leading eight cars. This locomotive was one of one hundred and eleven K4s constructed in 1918, by far the largest amount the Pennsy assembled in any given year. By 1954, southern New Jersey had become one of the few places on the entire PRR where a significant amount of passenger steam power remained in daily use.
(All - Frank C. Kozempel)

JORDAN, like **JERSEY**, was one of those very photogenic locations which could provide a safe and enjoyable location at which to view the passing parade of trains.

(Above) On Sunday, May 9, 1954, five-car New York – Atlantic City Train #1073 sails into the graceful curve behind PRR ES-15ms (EMD GP-7) #8553. This unit was assigned to a Trenton – Camden commuter run on weekdays, but on Sundays and holidays it was the usual power on Trains 1073 and 1078 instead of a PRSL unit. Built in September 1953, it is less than a year old here. *(Frank C. Kozempel)*

(Left) The Pennsy was justifiably proud of its Atlantic City service, as this 1904 timetable cover indicates. This through route was only in use for seven years at this time, and its most productive years were yet to come. *(William J. Coxey Collection)*

(Above) Train #1016 kicks up the snow as its two Budd cars round the curve below **JORDAN**, as seen from the Pennsy's Pemberton Branch bridge. Maple Avenue crosses in the background. It's February 20, 1966, and these cars are new to this route. Not all Atlantic City – Philadelphia trains were assigned RDCs, as they were still needed on two Camden – Millville round trips. A Sunday-only run, #1016 was the first train of the day from Atlantic City, due in 30th Street Station at 12:27 p.m.

(Right) A week later, on February 27, it's warm inside the cab as the 6016 propels Train #1011 into the curve just south of **JORDAN**. In about an hour the train will be easing to a stop in Atlantic City. This locomotive was one of ten Baldwin model AS-16 units (PRSL class BS-16ms #6007 through 6016) placed in service in 1953. In addition to steam generators and MU control, these units were equipped with two control stands so the locomotive could be operated with equal ease (and keep the engineer on the proper side) no matter which way the unit was facing. All of the PRSL's road switchers (EMD GP-38s as well) came with this option that eliminated the need to turn engines at the end of their run, saving time and money, the latter always in short supply on the PRSL. *(Above – Steven W. Tilden, right – William M. Tilden)*

Atlantic City Race Trains

"The Sport of Kings!" Such was the regard held for thoroughbred horse racing. Race tracks abounded in the Middle Atlantic states, luring the public to wager on the "win, place or show" of the horses. In the years just prior to and following World War II, many race courses were opened. Seasons, or "meets," were scheduled so that little conflict existed between tracks in a given area. They were a natural source of dependable traffic for the railroads since trains could be run, often in the "off" peak, from major cities directly to the "parks."

Atlantic City Race Course opened in 1946 and the following year it was served by a 3.2 mile branch from the main line near Cologne. Service was provided by a daily except Sunday round trip each from Philadelphia and New York via Delair, with an additional Philadelphia train on Saturday. The New York trains ceased in 1955 due to low patronage and the Philadelphia service remained as described above through the end of the 1967 season.

Steam locomotives were the primary power for the trains through 1957 and since there was no wye or servicing facilities located at the race track, the engines were coupled together and run light to Atlantic City for turning and servicing. The sight of three K4s on a Saturday sprint to Atlantic City was truly awesome!

Diesels were the sole power beginning in the 1958 season. Pennsy Alco PA-1 as well as EMD E-7 and E-8 units gave way to PRSL Baldwins up until the final runs in 1967 when a few pairs of Pennsy EFP-15 (EMD FP-7) units also were assigned, primarily to the second train on Saturdays. About ten of these units worked in the Philadelphia area that year on secondary freights and transfer runs. Fifteen years old at the time, they had originally been PRR #9832 through 9871, and had been renumbered 4332 through 4371 for the upcoming PRR/NYC merger.

While considered as PRSL trains, the Pennsy influence was quite obvious. In addition to being frequently hauled by PRR power, both in steam and diesel eras, they also utilized Pennsy coaches on occasion and refreshment (bar) cars.

(Above) The weekday train with the freshly-painted 6016 has a refreshment car mid-train in this September 13, 1967, view from the Maple Avenue bridge in Pennsauken. Since this was the final year for these trains, Penn Central never got involved in the venture.

(Below) This is the Saturday train on August 19, 1967, taken at Westmont from the Maple Avenue overpass, with the 4354 and 4368 in the lead. One of the final uses in passenger service for this class (EFP-15), they performed admirably and were a fitting way to end twenty-one years of service to the Atlantic City Race Course.
(Both – John P. Stroup)

(Left) Each summer the railroad advertised the Atlantic City race trains in newspapers and via "flyers" such as this 1957 issue, which were available at the Philadelphia stations.
(William J. Coxey Collection)

The other race track that was served from Philadelphia by train was Garden State Park, midway between **JORDAN** and Haddonfield. This was strictly a PRR operation. The race track opened in 1942, received its first train in 1946, and saw the last one in 1962. There were two annual "meets" here, spring and fall, which bracketed the longer summer one at the Atlantic City race track. The block station controlling access to the sidings at the Garden State race course was appropriately named **RACE** and was the only other point of note along the Bridge Branch.

As the 1960's wound down and seashore patronage dropped drastically, the PRSL received permission to discontinue all service into Philadelphia in 1969. The 6016 would haul the last locomotive-drawn PRSL passenger train, #1022, to Philadelphia on September 30, 1969. Thereafter the connection with the Patco High-Speed Line at Lindenwold would have to do for Philadelphia travelers.

(Right) This sunset on the Bridge Branch at **DIVIDE** interlocking in Delair on October 10, 1966, would signify what would happen three years later as the once busy artery from Philadelphia would only see the passage of an occasional local freight for another twenty years until Amtrak (and later New Jersey Transit) would begin renewed service. *(Steven W. Tilden)*

COLLINGSWOOD

(Left) Backtracking just a bit up the main line to include the suburban community of Collingswood, this is the first stop on the original 1853 route of the Camden and Atlantic. During the PRSL era, only local trains stopped here, en route to Haddonfield, Ashland or Hammonton, with one exception. Atlantic City – Camden express #106 began making a Collingswood station stop in the summer of 1955. This was the only seashore train to stop here, a practice that continued to the 1966 end of service. By the time of this February 9, 1964, scene, this station building was the only one between Camden and Haddonfield, as both Cuthbert Road and Westmont were merely shelters. The construction of the Patco Lindenwold High-Speed Line in 1966 spelled the end for this structure as well as the six miles of railroad itself. Collingswood and Westmont were moderately important commuter stops for the PRSL; when the High Speed Line was completed they would prove to be the same for that operation as well.
(John P. Stroup)

PRSL TRAIN NUMBER GROUPINGS

So far, the Philadelphia and New York trains have been our primary focus. However, shortly there will be quite a variety of train numbers appearing. To eliminate some confusion, the table below shows terminal points for PRSL train number series:

100 series:	Camden – Atlantic City
200 series:	Tuckahoe – Ocean City
300 series:	Camden – Wildwood
400 series:	Wildwood Jct. – Cape May
500 series:	Camden – Haddonfield, Ashland
600 series:	Camden – Clementon, Hammonton
700 series:	Camden – Millville
1000 thru 1040 series:	Phila. – Atlantic City
1050 and 1060 series:	Phila. – Wildwood
1070 and 1080 series:	New York – Atlantic City

Note: the 100 and 300 series were changed from Camden to Lindenwold in 1969.

MAIN LINE

Interlocking	Interlocking Station	Block Station	Block-Limit Station	STATIONS	Dist. from Camden	Sidings Assign. direc'n Car capacity 50 ft. cars		
						North	South	Both
X	X			CAMDEN				
				ALAN	0.4			
X	X	X		BROADWAY	0.6			
				CENTER	1.0			
				COLLINGSWOOD	4.1			
				CUTHBERT	4.8			
				WESTMONT	5.4			
				WEST HADDONFIELD	6.0			
X	X	X		JERSEY	4.8			
				DISTRICT POST (Phila. District)	4.9			
				DIVIDE				
				JORDAN				
				RACE				
				DISTRICT POST (Atl. Dist.) 969 feet North of Vernon Interlocking Station				
X	X	X		VERNON	6.0			
				HADDONFIELD	6.5	27		
				WOODCREST	8.6			
				ASHLAND	9.5		14	
				OSAGE	10.2			
				KIRKWOOD	11.2			
				LINDENWOLD	12.3			
				LUCASTON	13.5	30		
				WEST BERLIN	14.9			
				REED CROSSING	15.7			
				BERLIN	16.2		12	
				BISHOPS BRIDGE	17.3			
				ATCO	18.8	15	11	
				DUNBARTON	20.4			
				FISHER	21.0			
				CHESILHURST	21.8			
				WATERFORD	22.5	17		
				ANCORA	24.5			
X	X	X		WINSLOW	26.9			
			B	HAMMONTON	30.0		51	
				ELWOOD	36.2			
				EGG HARBOR	41.1	33		
				GATE	44.0			
				POMONA	46.3			
				ABSECON-Pleasantville	51.8			
				PENRED	56.2			
B	B	B		ATLANTIC	57.6			
				ATLANTIC CITY	57.9			

Distance between—
  District Post (Phila. Dist.) and Jordan........2.1
  Jordan and Race..........................1.8
  Race and Vernon..........................2.1
  District Post (Phila. Dist.) and Minson........1.0
  Minson and Jordan........................2.7

X—indicates in service continuously.
B—indicates in service part time.

WEST HADDONFIELD   VERNON

West Haddonfield station was at the junction of the PRR's Bridge Branch and the PRSL's mainline. The interlocking was controlled by **VERNON** tower, just across Mount Vernon Avenue from the station. Only Camden commuter trains stopped here, but it was another favorite spot to observe and photograph the action.

(Above) On July 11, 1954, nine-car Train #1078 is led by ten-month old PRR ES-15ms (EMD GP-7) #8553 as it passes **VERNON** tower en route to Trenton and New York. This lengthy mid-summer consist is the Sunday train which utilized PRR power (mostly the 8553) until 1961 when the New York–Atlantic City service was discontinued.

(Right) Years later, in January 1966, operator Elmer Green is busy at work inside **VERNON**, as he annotates the block sheet with the 4:01 p.m. time of #1022's passage. This was during the last month of **VERNON**'s use as a block station, as the Patco Lindenwold High-Speed Line construction continued to progress. *(Above – Frank C. Kozempel, right – Robert L. Long)*

WEST HADDONFIELD

The platform at West Haddonfield was a fine place to watch the show, as trains off the Bridge Branch fought their way around a curve and up out of "the hole" beneath Haddon Avenue to attain the level of the main line from Camden. These scenes aptly depict such struggles with heavy summer consists.

(Above) Reading class G-3 #218 has the seven cars of #1057 rolling grandly by on July 3, 1955. A word about these magnificent machines: during 1948, Reading Company constructed the last Pacific-type locomotives built in the U.S., #210 through 219, at their famed Reading, PA, shops. Unfortunately, their days were numbered almost immediately, as the Reading purchased six EMD FP-7 diesels in 1950 and two more in 1952.

Purchases in 1951 and 1952 of boiler-equipped road switchers from Baldwin, Alco and EMD completed dieselization of passenger service effective in May 1952. (Some Fairbanks-Morse TRAIN MASTER diesels purchased in 1953 and 1955 also had boilers.) Meanwhile, all but one of the G-3s found a home on the PRSL through 1955. #212 was damaged in a derailment on the Reading and was not repaired.

(Below) PRR K4s #3674 struggles to bring its fourteen-car race train up out of "the hole." Constructed in 1918, this locomotive saw service through two world wars, the Korean conflict, and was still going strong on September 4, 1954! Truly a testimony to the competent designers and craftsmen of that by-gone era. *(Both – Frank C. Kozempel)*

(Right) On Labor Day, September 6, 1954, the second section of the race train has double-headed K4s Pacifics for its heavy sixteen-car train, filled to capacity due to the holiday. The 3674 and 7133 team up for this spectacle of steam at West Haddonfield. The horse racing fans should arrive at the Atlantic City Race Course with time to spare as this pair of iron horses will race them south at full gallop once out of Haddonfield.

(Below) Displaying a much more leisurely gait, Reading G-3 Pacific #215 and a Reading coach represent Train #665 for Hammonton on August 6, 1954, on the mainline from Camden. Usually this train was assigned a single RDC; however, during the summer of 1954 all twelve Budd cars were utilized daily in Camden service to Ocean City, Wildwood and Cape May.
(Both – Frank C. Kozempel)

(Above) Having made the journey along the Pennsy's mainline and the Bridge Branch, the Philadelphia trains finally reach home rails at **VERNON** tower in West Haddonfield. Here at Mount Vernon Avenue, Train #1011 with its full summer consist is powered by #6015 on June 22, 1963. It's 11:45 a.m., and in exactly one hour the several hundred travelers aboard will be detraining in Atlantic City.

(Below) On Saturday, August 14, 1965, a race train headed up by the 6010 and 6025 approaches the Redman Avenue crossing south of **VERNON**. A concrete railroad telephone booth is seen to the right, and after the train passes the watchman will return, ironically, to his nearby wooden shanty. *(Above – John P. Stroup, below – William M. Tilden)*

The PRSL utilized its RDCs in almost all services envisioned by the Budd Company. The split of a single train into separate trains for various seashore destinations was a well known cost-saving operation. But the use of the cars in commuter service to Millville and Hammonton went largely unremarked. Hammonton locals via Haddonfield made twenty-one intermediate stops before completing their runs halfway to the shore, thirty miles later. Most of these stops were about one mile apart; the quick acceleration of the Budd Car enabled the schedule to be maintained, a testimony to the RDCs' excellent design.

(Above) In June of 1957, a Budd RDC protects the schedule of Hammonton local #655 as it rolls across Euclid Avenue in Haddonfield. As the RDCs were very economical to operate, the PRSL deadheaded some trains to enable a second revenue run with the same crew and car. By 1958 rather than lay over #655's RDC in Hammonton until the next morning, the car was quickly deadheaded to Haddonfield to operate as Train #522, the Camden connection from Philadelphia Train #1022. Then the same RDC would be used to make a second outbound commuter trip.

(Below) Not all special moves involved Atlantic City. This is the BANCROFT EXTRA, a sleeper movement to Maine, reposing on the Haddonfield public delivery siding in May 1958. The Bancroft School, serving mentally handicapped individuals, utilized rail service to transport residents between Haddonfield and their summer camp in Owl's Head, Maine. The nearest station to the camp was Rockland, which lost rail service in the late 1950s after a hurricane washed out a portion of the branch. This 1958 movement was likely the last. *(Both – William J. Coxey)*

HADDONFIELD

Haddonfield, established before the time of the American Revolution, was an important crossroads prior to the coming of the Camden and Atlantic Railroad in the early 1850s. Many fine homes and other buildings still exist here from the founding of our nation.

(Above) The 1867 station was once a source of pride here, and although by the 1960s its building and grounds were not as well-kept as they once were, it provided another attractive location for train watching. Even in winter, many fine scenes were recorded here, as evidenced on this cold night in February 1964.

(Opposite page, top) Train #1011 with the 6024 as power slowly grinds to a stop in March 1960. Despite the heavy snowfall, #1011 arrived right on the advertised –11:42 a.m. Delair Bridge openings, not the weather, were the principal cause of late running on the PRSL.

(Opposite page, bottom) It's February 17, 1964, and RDC #M402 prepares to leave as Train #508 for Camden. Having connected with #1008 from Atlantic City to Philadelphia, the engineer awaits the conductor's "highball" for the scheduled 9:31 a.m. departure. Through the late 1950s this was a popular train for Philadelphia department store patrons, professional people and their clients, often carrying over fifty passengers. By 1964, however, there are but a handful of riders. *(Above – Robert L. Long, opposite page, top – William J. Coxey, opposite page, bottom – John P. Stroup)*

27

The train activity continued to bustle in Haddonfield during the summer.

(Left) Nine of the twelve PRSL RDCs, running as Train #322, are slowing for the Haddonfield stop on Labor Day of 1956, in a scene which surely warmed the hearts of Budd Company personnel. This was on the last day of the summer season schedule and the railroad was responding to the extra-heavy demand on its service with equipment utilization such as this.

(Below) The 6013 slows for the stop with Train #1022 on June 27, 1965, during the last summer that this view will be possible. Construction of the Patco Lindenwold High-Speed Line the next year obliterated the entire scene forever.

(Opposite page, top) In a photo taken exactly two weeks earlier, the 6024 propels Train #1022 away from its 3:59 p.m. stop and on toward its arrival at 30th Street Station, Philadelphia, thirty-three minutes later.

(Opposite page, bottom) Here is truly a "moment in time," as Train #508 departs Haddonfield, with RDC #M403. Framed between an awning on a store front and a grand old tree, the activity near the station is caught on a fine day in August 1959. The Ford Motor Company was certainly well represented along the street. *(Above – William J. Coxey, below – Steven W. Tilden, opposite page, top – John P. Stroup, opposite page, bottom – Albert T. Holtz)*

(Above) Reading G-3 #214 is turning on the wye just south of the Haddonfield station, on the remnant of a former branch to Medford that had been abandoned in 1931. This is another example of the summer use of locomotive hauled trains to replace RDCs reassigned to seashore service. What a waste of a fine locomotive!

(Below) After the 214 has retrieved its Reading coach, it heads back to the station to operate as Train #522 to Camden on July 23, 1954.

(Opposite page) Not all of the Reading Pacifics were of the G-3 class. These were merely the last of the fine 4-6-2s that the Reading supplied to the PRSL. Prior to that, other Pacifics carried on the time-honored tradition established during Atlantic City Railroad days when the Reading forwarded train after train to the shore on their double-track Clementon route. Harking back to those days, here is G-2sa #178 (Baldwin, 1926; rebuilt by Reading, 1947) on Train #133, THE BOARDWALK FLYER, flying through Haddonfield, also on July 23, 1954. Train #133 was the PRSL's fastest run, carded to make the 57.9 mile trip in fifty minutes, with a stop at Absecon-Pleasantville.
(All – Frank C. Kozempel)

(Left) A large volume of traffic was attracted to the Reading's Atlantic City Railroad in spite of the austere appearance of their timetables, when compared to the Pennsy's. The entire series of Reading public timetables had a similar appearance. After 1933, the PRSL's own timetables would continue in this fashion until the adoption of the RDC image in 1970. *(William J. Coxey Collection)*

The curve immediately south of Haddonfield station provided numerous opportunities to show PRSL trains at their finest.

(Opposite page) On September 6, 1954, K4s #5495 thunders by with five Reading coaches as Train #1053, a mid-morning summer-only Wildwood express. After Frankford Junction, the next scheduled stop was Wildwood. Not only were locomotives supplied in the summer from the Pennsy and the Reading, passenger coaches were as well. Pennsy coaches assigned to commuter service could be deadheaded in from as far west as Pittsburgh for a weekend. Some cars could be spared in the summer when demand was lower due to vacationing workers and seasonal manufacturing shutdowns. The Reading likewise could spare cars from its Philadelphia commuter area, but in far less numbers.

(Above) Train #331, utilizing five RDCs, accelerates from Haddonfield station on a hot August day in 1957. This train was destined for Wildwood, with two cars for Ocean City and one for Cape May.

(Left) In contrast, winter's bite is in the air as mid-morning Atlantic City Train #1011 forges south in February 1958. There was still enough demand for year-round service, but shortly the railroad would begin its long process to eliminate as much passenger service as possible.
(Opposite page – Frank C. Kozempel, this page, both – William J. Coxey)

We move into the 1960s as we conclude our visit to this area.

(Above) Northbound Train #1056 with the 6015 is moments away from its 5:06 p.m. stop at the Haddonfield station on June 26, 1965. This Saturday-only summer train from Wildwood, Cape May and Ocean City is making its second run of the season.

(Left) The golden days of PRR Tuscan Red are relived in September 1960 as a race train splits the signals with EP-20 (EMD E-7) #5852 leading. In use for five summer seasons, these mainline locomotives were a welcome change from the usual black road switchers that had taken over from steam.
(Above – Steven W. Tilden, Left – William J. Coxey)

KIRKWOOD

South of Haddonfield, the towns are not as close together and the area becomes more rural. Having passed through Woodcrest, Ashland and Osage, the railroad actually travels through many undeveloped areas. One such spot is at Kirkwood, about five miles south of Haddonfield, where these winter scenes were recorded on February 11, 1964.

(Top) Southbound #1001, with the 6011 as power, blasts through at 9:15 a.m., en route to Atlantic City.

(Center) Return trip #1022 is shown at 4:35 p.m. as the storm diminishes. These two trains were among the most photographed in the PRSL's last few years, due to their scheduled times. They could also provide for a good day trip to Atlantic City with a five and one-half hour layover, providing plenty of time to photograph scenes around the station and engine facilities.

(Bottom) About a mile down the line in Lindenwold, a very late-running Saturday race train rolls along at a leisurely pace through the woods with substitute power, PRR EFS-17m (EMD GP-9) #7074 on October 7, 1967. This is during the last season of train service to the Atlantic City Race Course and the two EFP-15 (EMD FP-7) units were the usual power on this, the second of two trains. The first train each Saturday generally was assigned two PRSL Baldwin units. Apparently neither the EFP-15s nor a PRSL diesel was available, hence this unusual use of a freight unit. The passengers are no doubt anything but happy, as they will miss at least the first race of the day.
(Top and center – Robert L. Long, bottom – William M. Tilden)

LINDENWOLD

(Above) On July 2, 1969, Train #1057 utilizing RDCs M408 and M406 pulls away from the six month old Lindenwold station stop. On October 1st this would become the northern terminus for all PRSL seashore passenger trains, requiring travelers to change trains. The high-tech Patco High-Speed Line looms in the background. This change resulted in a further drastic reduction in ridership, nearly a fifty percent drop within six months. The scene would disappear forever after June 30, 1982 as the last former-PRSL passenger trains left Lindenwold for Atlantic City. Seven years later both Amtrak and New Jersey Transit would re-establish Atlantic City service after investing millions of dollars in station, track and signal improvements – a complete rebuilding of the line.

(Below) Budd Company equipment dominates the scene as the lone RDC awaits Atlantic City passengers at Patco's Lindenwold terminal in February 1969. Above, the Budd-built Patco cars are ready to depart for Philadelphia, during their first month of service to the "City of Brotherly Love."
(Above – John P. Stroup, below – Robert L. Long)

WEST BERLIN

Berlin and Atco are the only towns of any significance between Lindenwold and Hammonton, a distance of almost eighteen miles.

(Above) Engine #6008 is seen with an Atlantic City train passing through West Berlin, about two and a half miles south of Lindenwold in February 1968. In spite of much lower patronage, winter service to Atlantic City was operated primarily due to the political clout of the resort.

(Below) In October 1963, maintenance-of-way camp cars are on the siding at Berlin. Converted from former box cars, this equipment accompanied system track crews all over the railroad providing basic services for the gangs as they "camped" near their work site. Most railroads outfittted these cars for use as dormitories, kitchens, dining, recreation and storage for supplies and tools. Just one more facet of railroading that has vanished forever.
(Both – Robert L. Long)

BERLIN

(Top) The Berlin station, shown on February 20, 1964, served as a part-time block station as well as a ticket office. However, the agent's primary duty was handling the Atlantic City line's largest freight customer, the Owens-Corning pipe insulation plant in Berlin.

(Center) Inside, the only concession to modern times is the heater, which replaced the original pot-bellied stove. The agent's Thermos bottle is a recent touch, too, as he works on this April day in 1969.

(Bottom) Train #125 left Lindenwold at 5 p.m., and now scoots south below Berlin on February 22, 1970, while the winter sun hastens toward the horizon. The Budd Company rail diesel cars (RDC-1) were acquired after the PRSL arranged with the Budd Company for a demonstration run utilizing car #2960 that duly impressed invited members of the New Jersey Public Utilities Commission. The railroad saw these cars as an opportunity to lower operating costs as well as a chance to honor an earlier PUC mandate to upgrade the equipment in commuter service. Forty P-70 coaches had already been refurbished by the PRR, so the PUC agreed that purchasing twelve RDCs would serve the same purpose as having the remaining twenty coaches of the agreement renovated. As it turned out, this proved to be a real blessing for the railroad, as the cars provided over thirty years of low cost service.
(Top – John P. Stroup, center – Robert L. Long, bottom – Joseph J. Grella)

BISHOPS BRIDGE

(Above) It's a brilliant early fall day, September 30, 1967, at Bishops Bridge, midway between Berlin and Atco. PRR 4367 and 4347 are definitely pushing their 75 mph limit, as this race train blasts through. The Saturday train of one week before (page 35, bottom) certainly wasn't up to this effort. The EFP-15 units were the last "touch of class" to power PRSL trains. In two years the railroad would wind down locomotive-hauled passenger service and rely entirely on its small fleet of ten remaining RDCs.

(Right) Shortly behind the race train, the 6007 leads CA-289 past at a more leisurely pace. Even the freight service pictured here would soon change as the first group of GP-38s arrived from EMD in January.
(Both – John P. Stroup)

ANCORA

Proceeding toward the coast, pine forests encroach upon the railroad in the increasingly sandy soil. Population is sparse in this area, and the few human-generated sounds come from an occasional passing train and the steady flow of motor vehicle traffic on parallel U.S. Route 30, the White Horse Pike.

(Left) It's CA-289 once again, this time on September 10, 1966. The 6010 is rolling its train south just above Ancora, about six miles south of Atco, having passed through the barely noticeable villages of Dunbarton, Fisher, Chesilhurst and Waterford.

(Below) Shortly after CA-289 has passed, a Saturday race train sweeps around the Ancora curve and beneath the Route 30 bridge, with the 6011 and the 6013 for power. It's locations such as this which let the railroad fully utilize the potential of its passenger power. The 6000 through 6005 were rated for 65 mph, the 6007 through 6010 could reach 70 mph, but the real speedsters were the 6011 through 6016 and 6024 through 6027 which were geared for 80 mph! Of course the PRSL right-of-way was designed and maintained to allow this high-speed operation. *(Both – William M. Tilden)*

(Above) The 6012 has #1016 rushing north through Ancora on September 5, 1966. It should reach Haddonfield on time at 11:55 a.m. Concurrent to the massive reconstruction in Camden and the rerouting of some PRSL services to accommodate the Patco Lindenwold High-Speed Line, another large-scale PRR and PRSL project was in progress. This was the gradual single-tracking of the route between **JERSEY** tower and Atlantic City via the PRR's Bridge Branch and the PRSL mainline. Aside from a portion of the Millville Branch between **CENTER** tower and North Woodbury, by September 1966 the PRSL's last remaining double-track line was between Kirkwood and Absecon. Passenger schedules, the primary activity here, had declined to the point that the expense of retaining two tracks could not be justified. The Winslow – Absecon portion was single-tracked the following summer and the section between Kirkwood and Winslow followed suit in 1969.

(Right) Fifty years earlier, the railroad could barely handle the demand for its services. The cover of this 1916 timetable illustrates the boardwalk in Atlantic City, once more showing how the railroad and the resort were dependent upon one another. In ten short years this concept would be changed forever when the Delaware River Bridge opened from Philadelphia to southern New Jersey. *(Above – Steven W. Tilden, right – Robert J. Yanosey Collection)*

Ancora was the site of the last track pan (or trough) in southern New Jersey which supplied water to passing trains. The emphasis here is on passing. When steam locomotives needed to replenish their supply of water to provide steam, they usually had to stop and use a standpipe from a nearby tank. This, of course, interrupted the schedule and could add many minutes to the timetable. Long used on the Pennsy's main lines, this alternative method utilized troughs between the rails which were kept filled from a nearby tank. Some PRR road locomotives were equipped with a scoop attached to the bottom of the tender; the fireman manually lowered and raised the scoop for the purpose of filling the tender tank.

(Above) Just such an event is occurring in 1954 as a K4s takes a drink. But as Bob Long noted: "Scooping water – probably too fast! When I saw that water shooting out, I grabbed my cameras and got out of the way!"

(Below) This is more like it, as K4s #1139 takes water on June 27, 1954. The eight-car train is one of several Shriners Specials for a convention in Atlantic City and carried representatives from the SPHINX TEMPLE. Use of the Ancora pans was discontinued on August 10, 1954.
(Above – Robert L. Long, below – Frank C. Kozempel)

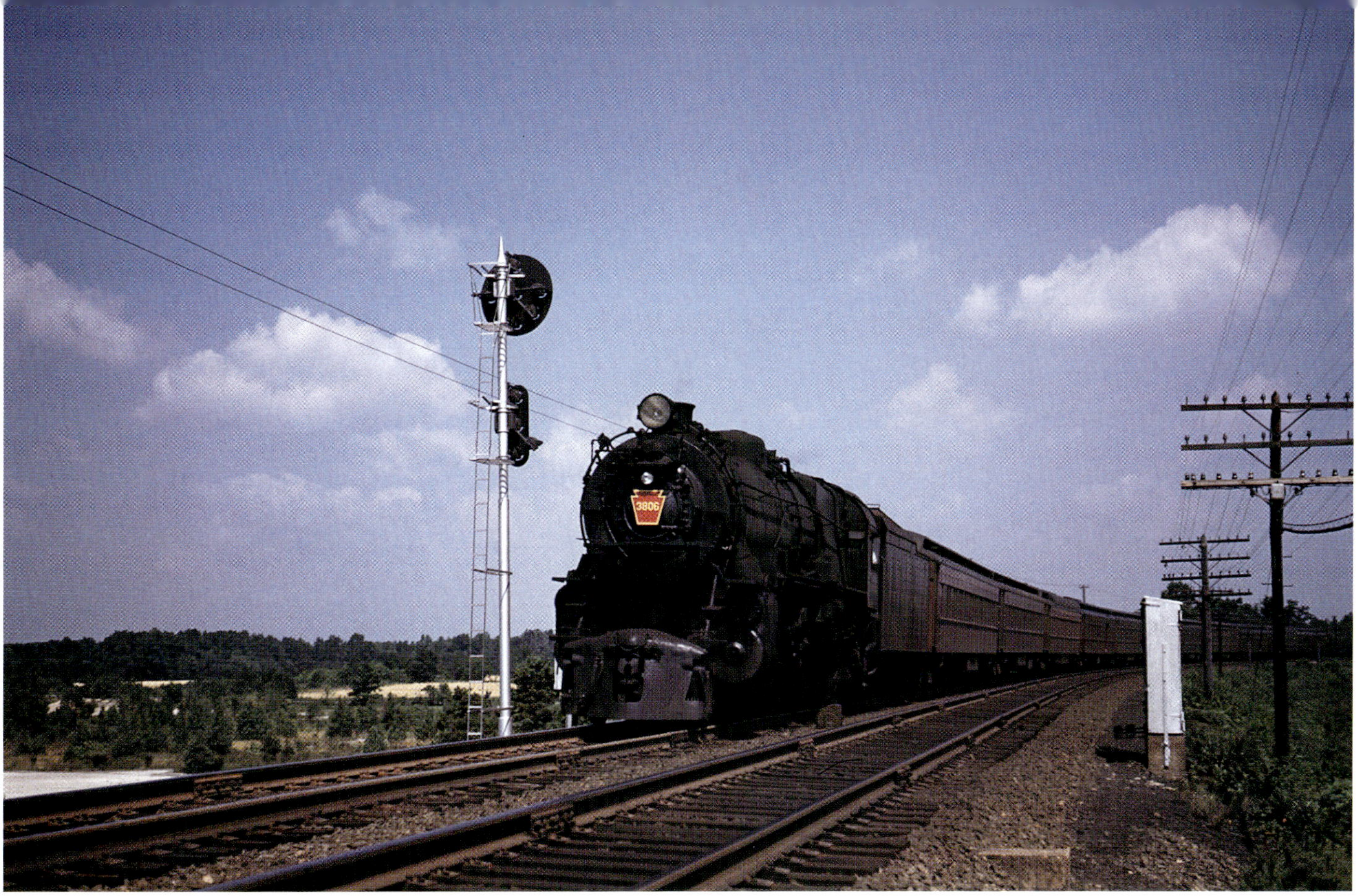

WINSLOW

About two miles past Ancora lies Winslow. In 1856, John L. Mason developed his MASON jars near here. Because of this, the fruits and vegetables of countless home gardens were preserved each autumn. More recently, clay bricks have been a major product for shipment out by rail.

WINSLOW

(Route map only, individual tracks not shown - JPS)

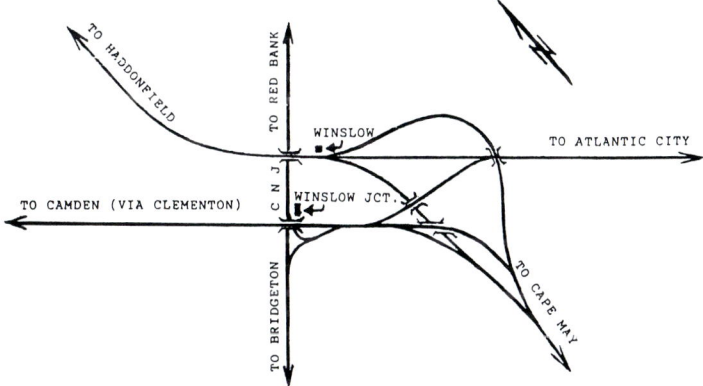

(Above) On June 27, 1954, Train #1057 is approaching **WINSLOW** tower with eleven cars behind K4s #3806, the engine involved in the Delair wreck of 1943. This Wildwood train will shortly diverge onto the Cape May Branch and accelerate southeast toward its next stop, at Tuckahoe.

(Right) **WINSLOW** tower, built in 1934 as part of the consolidation of facilities, sits high on the embankment overlooking the railroad junction in the middle of the pines, in this January 1967 view. Here the branches from Camden (via Clementon) and Cape May join the Atlantic City main line. Passing below under the bridge in the foreground is the Jersey Central's Southern Division running between Red Bank and Bridgeton. *(Above – Frank C. Kozempel, right – William J. Coxey)*

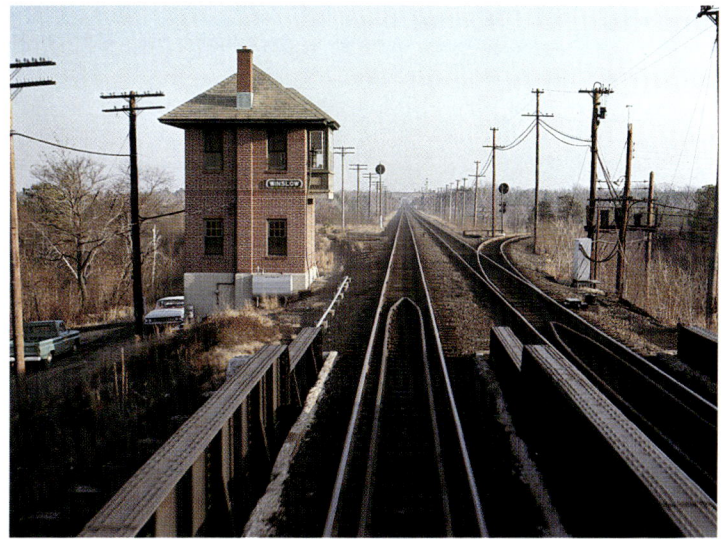

HAMMONTON

The first town of any size below Atco is Hammonton, three miles south of Winslow. Hammonton was founded in 1858 by Charles K. Landis, who would go on to greater fame as the father of Vineland. This was once the destination of a sizable number of local commuter trains which were gradually dropped until the final two round trips were discontinued in 1961. These Hammonton locals ran via both the main line and the Clementon Branch; some Atlantic City trains also stopped here. During the mid-50s Hammonton yard provided an opportunity to see the finest in 4-6-2 locomotives of both the Reading and the Pennsy.

(Above) On Sunday, June 27, 1954, four Reading G-3 locomotives are resting here: #215, 219 and 213, with the 214 behind. After turning on the wye, the engines were recoupled to their trains in the three-track yard. The Reading G-3s were put to good use in PRSL service, primarily in local service to Hammonton and on Wildwood expresses.

(Left) This August 7, 1955, scene belongs strictly to the Pennsy K4s. #5435, 7279 and 5418 show slightly different faces as they await the Monday morning call for Trains #606, 652 and 656 to Camden. During the summer of 1955, the Reading G-3s were used mainly on the Philadelphia – Wildwood trains.
(Both – Frank C. Kozempel)

In 1953, when the PRSL took delivery of #6011 through 6016, they came painted in ivy green, the color also used on building trim, station signs and elsewhere. Lettering and numbers were white. Unfortunately, this color scheme survived for only about two years. But fortunately, some of these locomotives were photographed prior to their receiving the standard PRSL black and yellow livery.

(Above) One such example is that of #6016 heading up four-car Train #1021 at Hammonton on November 29, 1954.

After the 1933 consolidation, there were a few segments of the Reading's Atlantic City Railroad that contained enough local business to warrant retention; these short portions of the once high-speed railroad were accessed from the parallel former PRR line by short connecting tracks.

(Right) One such segment was in Hammonton, shown here with local freight CA-295, powered by the 6028 on March 14, 1968. The final purchase of Baldwin products by the railroad occurred in 1956 when six more model S-12 switchers, 6028 through 6033, arrived. Unlike the five acquired in 1953, these came with MU capability, and as with all PRSL Baldwins, they quickly found a home in all types of service. *(Above – Frank C. Kozempel, right – John P. Stroup)*

(Below) The two Saturday race trains await the conclusion of the last race as they idle near the Atlantic City Race Course grandstand on September 10, 1966. #6012 and 6027 (left) and 6013 and 6011 pose during the next-to-last season by the twenty-year old facility. The race track, near the tiny crossroads named McKee City, was accessed from the Atlantic City mainline between Cologne and Pomona at **GATE** block station.

(Bottom) **TURF** block station was located at the other end of the 3.2 mile branch near the race track, as seen on September 10 also. Horse racing terms were appropriately used as names for these locations. Large group movements by the railroad such as this were a thrill to behold, as they performed a function which was ideally suited to the railroad's capabilities. Unfortunately by the mid-1960s, the cost of operation had nearly overtaken the revenue, which was declining each year, and the 1967 racing season proved to be the last in which the PRSL would participate.

(Below – Steven W. Tilden, bottom – John P. Stroup)

ABSECON

Continuing south on the mainline, the traveler passes through Egg Harbor City, developed around the Renault Winery (begun in 1870) and served by the two railroads whose main target was Atlantic City.

(Right) Next is Absecon, about twenty-two miles below Hammonton. The nearby town of Pleasantville had been served by the Reading's Atlantic City Railroad and when this route was abandoned during the 1933 consolidation the name was added to the Absecon stop. During a 1938 grade crossing elimination program, the railroad was elevated onto a nearly two-mile long embankment which necessitated construction of this masonry station, as seen here on February 27, 1964. In March 1962 a violent winter storm drove sea water all the way to Absecon and the resulting flood damage caused the PRSL to rebuild its line as single-track between here and Atlantic City.

(Below) Maintenance work required the assistance of PRR equipment at times, as seen on February 27 also, at Absecon. The work train consists of PRSL Burro crane MR-125, flat car #148 and PRR class N-6b cabin car #982416. Approaching is Train #1001 with engine #6011, just six miles from Atlantic City. *(Both – John P. Stroup)*

ATLANTIC CITY

Atlantic City had become one of the foremost seashore resorts in the United States by 1890. Aside from the beach, amusements, pageants and entertainment of all kinds were provided. Its convenience to the Philadelphia metropolitan area provided a "one-day round trip" concept as well as being the destination for millions of vacationers, but primarily in the summer. In fact, during much of the rest of the year, the railroads' huge investment in equipment and fixed plant lay practically idle. So too, were much of the city's hotel rooms and attractions. Atlantic City and the railroads did promote off-season activities with some success. There were national conventions, assorted sports shows such as ice skating, stage, screen and radio celebrity performances on Steel Pier and elsewhere, and of course, the Easter Parade on the boardwalk. Once many of New York's social elite rode parlor cars to Atlantic City, but the advent of highway travel gradually ended this patronage along with much of the coach business from Philadelphia.

As part of the PRSL consolidation process, completely new Atlantic City facilities were completed in 1934. The cost for the total terminal project was about four million dollars, the station itself costing a quarter million dollars. The new union station was located northwest of the original Reading station, the former site becoming a plaza in front of the new station.

(Above) This station is shown here in October 1955. The sad fate of this fine building would be to become the municipal bus terminal when the Atlantic City Expressway was opened ten years later.

After World War II, Atlantic City and the PRSL lost much of the huge throngs of summer day trippers and weekend vacationers from the Philadelphia area, as well as the year-round business. The downward spiral continued until eventually the last passenger train operated in 1982. Meanwhile, the casinos provided "pockets of prosperity," due to the passage of legalized gambling. Trains have returned, operated by Amtrak and New Jersey Transit, but most travelers enticed by the prospect of "the big win" either drive there themselves or arrive by bus, taken directly to the casinos.

(Left) Once private motor vehicles operated by the many prestigious hotels met each train to facilitate the completion of the traveler's journey. Here, in February 1965, the parking area is a silent reminder of those once opulent days of the thirties and forties.

(Above – Albert T. Holtz, left – Robert L. Long)

Although a private horse car line had been operating in Atlantic City along Atlantic Avenue since about 1865, the Camden and Atlantic built a double-track line on the same route from its South Carolina Avenue station to South Atlantic City in 1881. Three years later it was extended to Longport from the inlet, with the city portion being electrified in 1889, the remainder in 1893. While still retaining ownership, the PRR contracted with the Atlantic City and Shore RR Co. in 1907 to operate it, even into the PRSL era. In December 1939, the PRR placed an order with Brill Car Company of Philadelphia to replace the aging fleet of trolleys. This twenty-four car order was an attempt to help keep Brill afloat, an example of a Pennsy practice to patronize good customers and fellow home-town corporations. Brill had gone its own way, and not joined other car builders in producing the much more popular "PCC" car.

In December 1945 the PRR sold the trolley line to the newly-formed Atlantic City Transportation Company. In exactly ten years, the trolleys would be replaced by the omni-present GMC busses. In these October 1955 scenes, the "Brill-liners" are rolling their last miles.

(Top) Southbound car #224 heads down Atlantic Avenue; this route was shared with the cars of affiliated Shore Fast Line during the final years of that service to Ocean City.

(Center) As the cars were single-ended, they had to utilize turning loops at each end of the line, unlike the Shore Fast Line interurbans which were double-ended. Car #219 has turned on the loop and awaits departure time beside one of the replacement GMC busses.

(Bottom) Car #204 stops for riders along Atlantic Avenue enroute to Longport. In two months the "Miss America Fleet" will be history.
(All – Robert L. Long collection)

Certainly not what comes to most people's minds when they think of Atlantic City, these scenes depict the final years of steam, when Pennsy power was quite abundant here.

(Above) On September 18, 1954, an N.R.H.S. special has arrived, and its power, E-6s #460, is being turned. This class, which now consisted merely of #460, 645 and 1600, would soon be retired. In 1914, 80 E-6s locomotives were built, following extensive testing of a 1910 prototype and two more in 1912. The claim to fame of #460, and perhaps the entire class, was an exploit in 1927 which pitted a train against an airplane. When Charles Lindbergh made his triumphant return from Paris after becoming the first person to fly solo across the Atlantic Ocean, his Washington, D.C. arrival was filmed by newsreel cameras for presentation in movie theaters. A special PRR train powered by #460 made a dash to Manhattan Transfer just north of Newark, NJ, 216 miles in 175 minutes! The films that were developed on board were shown in New York theaters before those that were developed first and then sent by plane. Thus #460 would hereafter be referred to as the "Lindbergh engine." This Atlantic type would eventually become part of the PRR historical collection and later go to the Railroad Museum of Pennsylvania at Strasburg.

(Below) On Sunday, March 13, 1955, K4s 5497 lays over between runs. This Pacific was one of 425 K4s built between 1914 and 1928. Seventy-two still existed in 1956, and of these, twenty were still in service.
(Both – Frank C. Kozempel)

(Above) PRR B-6sb #6399 heads in on a station track to retrieve the cars from Train #1073, which had just arrived from New York. PRR ES-15ms (EMD GP-7) 8553 powered the train on this Sunday in October 1955. Even though the PRSL had received six Baldwin diesel switchers by this time, a few Pennsy steam switchers were still needed here and at other yards. The PRSL's own B-6sb locomotives were all retired by 1952.

(Below) In August 1960 the four-stall roundhouse was still standing, three years after seeing the last of the iron horses which required its services. This former Pennsy facility was kept in operation by the merged company since the former Reading facility was abandoned to make way for the new passenger terminal.

(Right) This map was provided on the back of the 1904 PRR timetable to acclimate the public regarding the location of the Pennsy's station in relation to main Atlantic City attractions. It also shows the Atlantic Avenue streetcar line which the Pennsy operated as a subsidiary to the West Jersey and Seashore Railroad.
(Above – Albert T. Holtz, below – William J. Coxey, right – William J. Coxey collection)

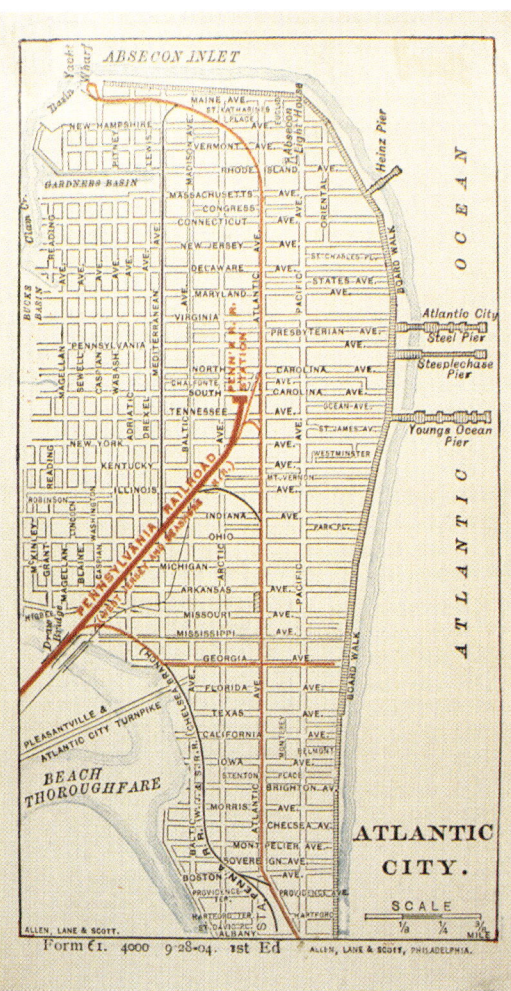

Some examples of Pennsy diesel power at Atlantic City are shown in August 1958.

(Above) AFP-20 (Alco PA-1) #5758 idles behind sister #5757 awaiting Monday morning's call to the two Camden commuter runs. This class of ten cab units and five booster units had been built in 1947 as class AP-20. Along with similar Baldwin, EMD, and Fairbanks-Morse passenger units, the Pennsy had acquired products from the various builders to dieselize their long-haul operations west of Harrisburg. Settling on EMD's E-units, the railroad went on to order a large quantity of model E-8A units to complete the task and standardize the fleet. Non-EMD power was downgraded for use on secondary runs and eventually commuter service; in 1952 the Alco PA-1s became class AFP-20, regeared for dual service – freight or passenger. By the late 1950s half of the fleet was in use in central Pennsylvania hauling coal trains (!) and the remainder was assigned to the Camden engine terminal to assist the power-hungry PRSL as well as the PRR's own needs: freight transfers to Philadelphia or northern New Jersey, troop trains to Fort Dix, or local passenger trains on the Bordentown and Pemberton Branches. By 1960 the 5752, 5753 and 5756 had joined their sisters and the booster units in Pennsylvania and 5757 and 5758 continued to work out of Camden until retirement in 1962.

(Left) Leased GS-4 (GE 44-ton) #9328 works yard job #70-A on the same Sunday afternoon. This was one of four GE units that the PRSL leased from the Pennsy. The others were 9326, 9327 and 9337, and all had been built in 1947 and 1948. They were assigned to replace the very small PRR class A-5 0-4-0 steam switchers which were needed on tight-radius curves of some industrial trackage, that in some cases also had light rail, located in Camden and Salem as well as Atlantic City. The GE units continued in this service into the early 1960s.

(Both – William J. Coxey)

NEWFIELD BRANCH   SOMERS POINT BRANCH

Built by a predecessor of the West Jersey and Seashore in 1880, the Newfield Branch became part of a through 65-mile, third-rail electric route from Camden to Atlantic City in 1906. It was a relief to the main line so as to accommodate as many people to the shore as possible. The final electric trains ran between Newfield and Atlantic City in 1931; the final passenger service, which consisted of an Atlantic City-based gas-electric rail motor car making two round trips, was withdrawn in 1950. Nine years later the Newfield – Mays Landing portion of the branch was abandoned, with the segment north of McKee City succumbing in 1966.

(Right) Seventeen miles to the West of Atlantic City is Mays Landing. Its station is shown on May 1, 1954, from the Route 50 overpass. Once situated on a busy double-track route, the residents of the Atlantic County seat had to settle for an occasional Public Service bus for public transportation. In the 1960s, this rail line and the adjoining Somers Point Branch were served by a twice weekly local freight out of Atlantic City.

The Somers Point Branch was also built in 1880; it became the route of the Shore Fast Line from downtown Atlantic City via Pleasantville to Somers Point, continuing across the bay into Ocean City. This electrified interurban began service in 1906, eventually folding in 1948. It was operated by the Atlantic City and Shore Railroad, as was the city streetcar line in Atlantic City. No railroad buildings existed on this line by the 1960s, and the portion south of Linwood was abandoned in 1966.

(Below) The Shore Fast Line issued colorful brochures to encourage travel to Ocean City via Somers Point. This excerpt was written to entice travelers aboard the orange interurbans.
(Photo – Frank C. Kozempel, brochure – Robert J. Yanosey collection)

NEWFIELD SECONDARY TRACK

Interlocking	Interlocking Station	Block Station	Block-Limit Station	STATIONS	Dist. from Camden	Sidings Assign. direc'n Car capacity 50 ft. cars		
						North	South	Both
				MAYS LANDING 4300 ft. North	47.7			25
				REEGA	51.4			
				McKEE CITY	53.9			20
				CARDIFF	55.8			
				MOUNT CALVARY	57.8			
				PLEASANTVILLE Cemetery	58.8			
				PLEASANTVILLE	59.3			50
				PENRED	62.8			
B	B	B		ATLANTIC	64.1			
				ATLANTIC CITY	64.4			

B—indicates in service part time.

SOMERS POINT SECONDARY TRACK

Interlocking	Interlocking Station	Block Station	Block-Limit Station	STATIONS	Dist. from Camden	Sidings Assign. direc'n Car capacity 50 ft. cars		
						North	South	Both
				PLEASANTVILLE	59.3			
				DOLPHIN	60.7			
				NORTHFIELD	61.1			
				BAKERSVILLE	61.7			
				LINWOOD	63.2			
				OCEAN HEIGHTS	65.0			
				SOMERS POINT	66.1			

A Sixteen Mile Ride Over the "Shore Fast Line's" Famous Scenic Route to Ocean City

One Day Round Trip Excursion 75¢

Fifty minutes spent in comfortable High Speed Electric cars carry you over the interesting meadowland through the charming communities of Pleasantville, Northfield, Linwood and Somers Point, riding for many miles thru the invigorating pines; then over Great Egg Harbor Bay into the sister resort of Ocean City with its two and one-half miles of Boardwalk lined with attractive shops, a beautiful bathing beach and hotels modern in every respect. Take cars at Virginia Ave. and Boardwalk, Atlantic City and at all street intersections on Atlantic Ave. between Virginia Ave. and Mississippi Ave.

WINSLOW

Returning to Winslow, we are now positioned for a journey down the Cape May Branch, with side trips to Ocean City and Wildwood. South of **WINSLOW** tower on the Cape May Branch is the connection with the Clementon Branch.

(Above) Here on July 7, 1970, is train CM-91, the Pavonia – Tuckahoe freight, behind the 2005 and 2006, waiting for the passage of RDC M405 running as Train #255.

(Below) A few minutes later CM-91 is on the move. Train #255 was a summer-only weekday train just to Ocean City, unique in the sense that it had no connections for Wildwood and Cape May. This was the first of three summer seasons for this train. As ridership seldom exceeded a dozen passengers per trip, it was not operated after the summer of 1972. Its weekend counterpart was the generally well-patronized Wildwood Train #357, which also served Ocean City and Cape May via connections.

(Opposite page, top) The next month, on August 22, Train #357 glides by with the M413 and M409.

(Opposite page, bottom) The last scene shows the passage of a Beesley's Point Extra on April 20, 1969, with the 2004-2005-2002 as power. The electric generating plant operated by Atlantic City Electric Company provided the railroad with a great source of revenue, as it required large amounts of coal as well as imported crude oil to keep its three boilers running. Sometimes the fuel would be included in the Cape May County freight, CM-91, but most often a separate train would be run, usually with two or three GP-38s, especially during times of peak demand for electricity.

(All – John P. Stroup)

TUCKAHOE

The line between Winslow and Tuckahoe was former Reading territory, first laid down in 1890. Running over twenty-five miles through pine forests and a few small towns, the trains crossed the Tuckahoe River and ground to a halt at the station. Here the last car or two was cut off the rear of most Wildwood trains for Ocean City. Sometimes passengers were required to change to a short train at Tuckahoe to make the run to Ocean City. The procedure was reversed on the trip from the shore. With Budd cars, connections got a bit easier, as each car had its own controls, and after uncoupling, each train went its separate way.

(Above) These scenes on August 27, 1966, show the combining of Train #256 from Ocean City into #1056 from Wildwood. Engine #6019 has left the coach from Ocean City by the station as #1056 is arriving in the background. Then #1056 will back onto the Ocean City Branch to pick up its connection.

(Opposite page, top) After adding the coach, #1056 leaves for Philadelphia behind the 6024, as engine 6019 sits on the siding. It will shortly deadhead back to Ocean City to handle evening Philadelphia connection #262. This was how it was done for over seventy-five years, most of that time behind steam. In three years the line would become the exclusive domain of the Budd cars.

(Opposite page, bottom) PRR EFS-17m (EMD GP-9) #7188 has arrived at Tuckahoe with CM-91 and splits the searchlight signals while on the Ocean City Branch. One could look forward to seeing PRR and Reading diesels make an occasional journey down here, especially in the summer when the PRSL's own units were busy handling extra passenger trains. The signals were installed in 1941 to replace the outmoded former Reading signals.

(All – William M. Tilden)

CAPE MAY, OCEAN CITY AND WILDWOOD BRANCHES

Interlocking	Interlocking Station	Block Station	Block-Limit Station	STATIONS		Dist. from Camden	Sidings Assign. direc'n Car capacity 50 ft. cars		
							North	South	Both
X	X	X		WINSLOW		25.9			
				FOLSOM		29.4			
				NEWTONVILLE		33.4			
				RICHLAND	CAPE MAY BRANCH	38.0			
				MILMAY		41.7			
				DOROTHY		44.4			
				RISLEY		46.7			
B	B	B		TUCKAHOE		53.3			
B	B	B		TUCKAHOE		53.3			39
				PETERSBURG		56.5			
				PALERMO		59.5			23
				CROOK HORN BRIDGE	OCEAN CITY BRANCH	61.8			
				51st STREET (Ocean City)		61.9			30
				34th STREET (Ocean City)		63.7			
				24th STREET (Ocean City)		64.8			
				14th STREET (Ocean City)		65.8			
			B	OCEAN CITY (10th Street)		66.3			
				WOODBINE JCT.–Woodbine		57.4			
				DENNISVILLE		60.7			23
				GOSHEN	CAPE MAY BRANCH	65.2			25
				CAPE MAY COURT HOUSE		68.3			40
				MAYVILLE		69.4			
				WHITESBORO		71.5			
			B	WILDWOOD JCT.		72.5			30
				GRASSY SOUND BRIDGE	WILDWOOD BR.	74.9			
				WEST WILDWOOD		75.3			
			B	WILDWOOD		76.5			
			B	WILDWOOD JCT.		72.5			30
				RIO GRANDE		73.8			15
				ERMA	CAPE MAY BRANCH	76.1			
				CANAL MOVABLE BRIDGE		78.1			
			X	HARBOR BRANCH JCT.		78.4			
			X	CAPE MAY		80.0			

X—indicates in service continuously.
B—indicates in service part time.

WOODBINE SECONDARY TRACK

Interlocking	Interlocking Station	Block Station	Block-Limit Station	STATIONS	Dist. from Camden	Sidings Assign. direc'n Car capacity 50 ft. cars		
						North	South	Both
				WOODBINE 1839 feet North of	56.8			
				WOODBINE JCT. 3950 feet South of	60.0			

(Left) **TUCKAHOE** tower was typical of thousands across the nation which were never modernized, retaining its "armstrong" lever rack that controlled the various nearby switches and signals. The junction was quite simple and consisted merely of a wye track between the two single-track branches with the station, freight house and water tank in the center and the tower located at the northern switch. It was a hot Saturday afternoon in August 1969 when this scene was taken, but it could easily have been fifty years earlier.

(Below) PRR 7188 has finished its work and is heading back to Pavonia with CM-90 on August 27, 1966. There will be one more train to combine here tonight, when #1062 picks up its Ocean City car and departs at 8:58 p.m. Then it will just be the incessant buzz of mosquitoes, prolific due to the nearby Tuckahoe River, to keep the operator alert until he locks up the tower at 9:30 p.m. and heads for home. In 1964 **TUCKAHOE** was reduced to a two-trick operation. This labor-saving change took place after the regular freight, CM-91/90, was rescheduled to run during the daytime. Due to the drastic reduction of passenger service in the 1960s, ample time existed during the day not only to run this freight but the Beesley's Point Extras as well.
(Left – William J. Coxey, below – William M. Tilden)

The Cape May Branch is still very much alive during the winter season, but the general public is little aware of that fact.

(Above) Engine 2004, working train CM-91, idles by the station as the crew grabs a bite to eat on March 27, 1968. Shortly they will couple to some empty tank cars brought earlier from Beesley's Point and head back to Pavonia Yard in Camden as train CM-90.

(Below) Traveling along the Ocean City Branch the day before, a Beesley's Point Extra, led by the 2002 and 2000, brings empties back from the generating station. Shown crossing the Cedar Swamp Creek between Petersburg and Palermo, it is about halfway between the power plant and Tuckahoe. Other than an occasional carload of lumber or jetty rock into Ocean City, coal and oil were the principal traffic on the branch.
(Both – John P. Stroup)

OCEAN CITY

In 1879 three Methodist ministers, the Lake brothers, founded Ocean City as an alcohol-free family resort. Five years later the West Jersey route built into town followed in 1897 by a railroad that would eventually become part of the Reading. This was an important year, as the community became an official city, completely owned by the Ocean City Association, which controlled all functions within the corporate limits. The next year a station was erected at 9th Street, later moved to 10th Street. The island's eight miles of beaches attracted visitors from far and wide, and Ocean City's status as a family resort was firmly in place.

Meanwhile the barrier islands stretching from Atlantic City south to Cape May were equally well situated for many other resort towns. Naturally the railroads attempted to serve each and every location, and the Pennsy and Reading predecessors each built nearly parallel lines along the coast. Hampered by occasional flooding and by the extremely seasonal business, they eventually retreated as highway travel developed until only lines to Ocean City, Wildwood and Cape May remained by the early 1950s. In some cases the railroad had to offer substitute bus service in order to gain permission to abandon their train service. Most of this "highway" operation was contracted to Public Service, long an arch-rival in the seashore trade, but a peaceful partner by the 1950s.

(Above) Three faces of Ocean City passenger railroading are shown here. The Public Service bus connection to Sea Isle City and Townsend Inlet is ready to leave from 51st Street, Ocean City. Here Train #211 makes the connection from Camden on a Saturday morning in August 1961. The train will terminate at 10th Street, Ocean City, in thirteen minutes, with the bus reaching Townsend Inlet after a run of twenty-four minutes.
(Above – Albert T. Holtz; emblem – John P. Stroup collection)

(Top) Train #257 with the 6028 and a single coach arrives at 14th Street, Ocean City in August 1959. The coach had been cut off at Tuckahoe from Philadelphia Train #1057 enroute to Wildwood.

(Center) The 6008 is arriving on time at 11:31 a.m. at 10th Street station in August 1961 with Train #257. This was the end of the Ocean City Branch in the 1960s, and was thirteen miles from Tuckahoe. The line made a rather long loop into town, entering from the south and included five stations for the convenience of patrons.

(Bottom) Another rail route into Ocean City consisted of the Shore Fast Line's service from Atlantic City via Somers Point until 1948. These excerpts from one of their brochures provided vacationers in either Atlantic City or Ocean City with the route and schedule so an interesting side trip could be planned.
(Top and center – Albert T. Holtz, bottom – Robert J. Yanosey collection)

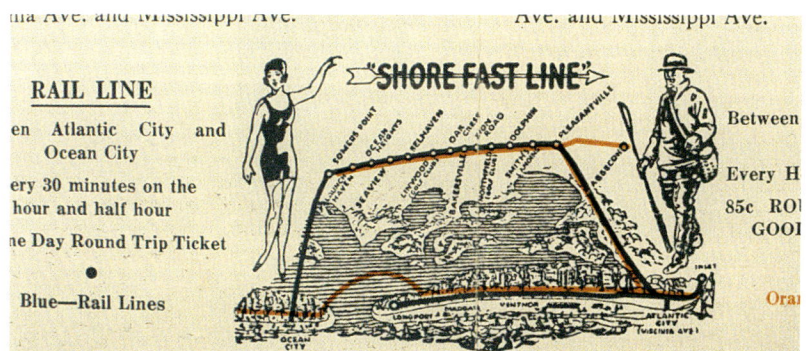

DENNISVILLE

(Above) Dennisville is located along the Cape May Branch, seven miles south of Tuckahoe. This station was built at the time the railroad reached here in 1894 and became the shipping point for cedar shingles produced from trees "mined" from nearby Cedar Swamp. Used primarily in southern New Jersey and eastern Pennsylvania, the shingles even found their way onto the roof of Independence Hall in Philadelphia. The industry had died out by the time of this July 27, 1954, scene, and trains no longer stopped here as they rushed travelers toward Wildwood and Cape May. Train #311 has left its Ocean City car behind at Tuckahoe and shortly will pass through Goshen, Cape May Court House, Mayville and Whitesboro, before "splitting" again at Wildwood Junction. At Cape May Court House, a bus connection accommodated travelers to Stone Harbor and Avalon, replacing the connecting train service from 1954 until ending finally in 1971.

(Left) From within Dennisville station, the stained glass windows still glowed brightly in July 1964. Many former Reading stations incorporated this feature.

(Right) This October 25, 1970, timetable design, for the first time featuring an RDC, would continue through the Conrail years into the New Jersey Transit era until the 1982 end of Atlantic City service. The "Philadelphia" origin was a bit misleading, as the Patco route was the only rail service north of Lindenwold.

(Above – Frank C. Kozempel, left – Robert L. Long, right – John P. Stroup collection)

WILDWOOD

Wildwood – the rogue of the South Jersey shore! From Ocean City to Cape May, the string of towns promoted the surf and sand as their primary, and often only, attraction. But not Wildwood. Started in 1890, it soon grew to rival Atlantic City for its gaudiness as well as naughtiness and eventually grew into a city of amusements, night clubs, glitz and neon. To be sure, Wildwood had a wonderful beach also; deep sea fishing was a huge draw too, as many charter boats operated out of Wildwood Yacht Basin and Cold Spring Harbor. It was served by both the PRR and a Reading-controlled connection, the Wildwood and Delaware Bay Short Line, which was completed in 1912.

(Above) Survivor of the PRSL consolidation, the more direct former Reading route utilized this rambling station at Oak Avenue up until the end of passenger service in 1973. It is shown on April 16, 1961, with RDC M413 to the right on the track constructed by the PRSL to connect with the former PRR line to Cold Spring Harbor, where a loop was located to turn steam locomotives. This arrangement would serve the railroad well in the steam era.

(Right) Reading G-1sa #130, a 1924 Baldwin product, is shown at Wildwood Crest in this undated scene. As the trains interfered with the ever-increasing automobile traffic south of Wildwood, the advent of diesel power and declining business led to the abandonment of the Cold Spring Harbor line in 1958, much to the relief of the town fathers.
(Above - John P. Stroup, right– Karl P. Then)

WILDWOOD JCT.

(Above) Train #1057, having left two cars at Wildwood Junction, has swung off toward the east, and Wildwood. Here the Cape May connection, Train #457, is leaving for Rio Grande, Erma and Cape May. In seven and a half miles Reading G-3 #211 will reach its destination on this July 27, 1954.

(Below) The cover of the 1937 PRSL brochure depicts "Barnacle Bill," and is an example of the railroad's attempt to lure fishermen onto a dedicated train. A great many took the bait. The excerpt from inside the folder extols the benefits of traveling directly to the charter boat docks.
(Above – Frank C. Kozempel, below – Robert J. Yanosey collection)

Here's the car(e)free way to go!

The Damocles sword of all fishing parties is the thought of scrambling from bed, in the wee small hours, and then—after a day's fun on the water—the tedious drive home, through heavy traffic. Fishing is a recreation done for the pleasure and enjoyment it offers. Why make a hardship of it? Thousands don't.

They take the FISHERMEN'S SPECIAL or the ATLANTIC CITY ANGLER, or even regular trains of the Pennsylvania-Reading Seashore Lines to south Jersey fishing points and reap the most from their holiday. They get up at a more reasonable hour. Responsibility to themselves or their buddies is eliminated. No blow-outs or engine trouble. No risk of smelling-up the family car or fatigue from driving through congested traffic. And best of all there is time to relax and play pinochle or bridge going and returning.

There is an added measure of enjoyment, too, when travelling via either of the two crack flyers operated for anglers. Your fellow passengers are fishermen, too. It's just like a fishing club, on wheels, speeding you direct to the docks, like the wind. The FISHERMEN'S SPECIAL runs from Philadelphia (Market Street Wharf) right to the dock at Schellenger's Landing in 100 minutes, Cold Spring Harbor in 110 minutes. The ATLANTIC CITY ANGLER takes you from Market Street Wharf in 75 minutes, with free buses waiting in Atlantic City to carry fishermen to the Inlet docks. Leave all car(e)s behind. Travel via the Pennsylvania-Reading Seashore Lines, the route of the FISHERMEN'S SPECIAL AND THE ATLANTIC CITY ANGLER.

CAPE MAY

Cape May predates all of the coastal resorts in southern New Jersey, even Atlantic City. Popular with New Yorkers and Philadelphians since 1766, it is the nation's oldest seashore resort. By the mid-nineteenth century it had become quite fashionable for those of high society to vacation there. The over six-hundred Victorian homes continue to be the focal point of Cape May, with four miles of beaches, a large marina and the landmark 1859 Cape May Point lighthouse as additional attractions.

Cape May was first reached by rail, via Millville, in 1863 and the Reading arrived in 1894. Freight traffic was not great, but in 1941 Northwest Magnesite Company began processing dolomite into magnesite at Cape May Point. This plant was the largest customer south of Winslow until the Beesley's Point generating station opened in 1962. By the mid 1960s the balance of the Cape May Branch traffic totaled about a dozen cars a day consisting mostly of building materials such as lumber inbound, and seafood products outbound.

(Above) The station here in Cape May, as well as at most seashore points, was not close to the ocean; most travelers would first take a taxi to their hotel upon arrival. Then they would head for the beach. On February 22, 1964, Budd car M413, locomotive 6002 and cabin car 235 share track space at the station.

(Right) The scene has changed by October 1970, as M411 and 2001 idle at Cape May, the southern-most point on the PRSL. Passenger service ended in 1981 and local freight WY-390/391 would have the railroad all to itself.
(Above – John P. Stroup, right – William J. Coxey)

> Having concluded our visit to the "seashore" areas of the railroad, we will now visit the balance of the PRSL, starting at Camden, the main base of operations.

Camden is an old city, connected with Philadelphia only by several ferryboat routes until 1926, when the Delaware River Bridge, the first direct connection, was completed. The Camden County seat was a manufacturing city, and home to various well-known enterprises, such as Esterbrook Pen Company (1858), Campbell Soup Company (1869), New York Shipbuilding Company (1899) and the Victor Talking Machine Company, a predecessor of RCA Victor (1901). Each of these companies was serviced directly by the PRSL; other than New York Shipbuilding, all of them were located north of the Pennsy's huge riverfront engine facility and yard.

(Above) At the Pennsy's Camden Terminal Enginehouse, PRR K4s and Reading G-3 Pacifics are ready on August 18, 1954, to take their assignments on the head end of PRSL passenger trains.

(Below) PRR E-6s #402 lays over in this undated scene, probably taken in 1948. Of the eighty-three machines of this class, many saw service on the PRSL, with nine formally transferred to the PRSL. They were familiar sights on the head end of PRSL passenger trains of all types, even after the Pennsy class K4s power came into prominence.

(Above - Frank C. Kozempel, below - Karl P. Then)

(Top) Five other 4-4-2s of the PRSL were of class E-3sd, formerly on the West Jersey and Seashore roster. The 6061, built new for the WJ&S in 1905 as an E-2a, was rebuilt to an E-3sd in 1919. It is shown forlornly awaiting the scrapper, having been stripped of its rods, headlight and other appurtenances. The other four of the class were retired in 1935 and 1938. However, this engine somehow survived for another ten years until scrapped in September 1948 along with the class E-6s locomotives during the following three years.

(Center) Laying over at Camden on November 21, 1948, is another steam-powered piece of equipment, a PRSL pile driver. Vital to the maintenance of the line's many wooden trestles, this machine would eventually join its locomotive brethren on technology's scrap heap.

(Bottom) All PRSL owned or leased locomotives, both steam and diesel, were maintained at the Camden Terminal Enginehouse until 1965 when the riverfront facilities were relocated to Pavonia Yard. Serving well for so many years, the now forever abandoned water tank and coaling tower stand silent on April 9, 1966. To the west, out of the picture to the left, was the site of the ferry terminal and its adjacent station.

 (Top and center – Karl P. Then, bottom – Steven W. Tilden)

(Above) Leaving the coach yard is the first Reading G-3, #210, with a matching train of Reading coaches. In this classic Camden scene, the J.B. VanSciver Furniture building dominates the background on this beautiful Sunday morning August 23, 1953. This is during the first year of the G-3s short stay on the PRSL, which would end in 1955.

(Below) A short while later, the action continues as another Reading G-3, this time the 215, rolls by. Nosing into the scene is one of the PRSL's class BS-15ms Baldwin road switchers. Beyond the Reading locomotive may be seen the abandoned ferry terminal at the foot of Federal Street. Not far from here, on Mickle Street, the poet Walt Whitman lived the last few years of his life. He often rode the ferries, perhaps gaining ideas for his work, before his death in 1892.

(Both – Ed Kelsey)

About a city block to the east, Pennsy 4-6-2 locomotives are shown performing on the same stage.

(Above) On a crisp, clear January afternoon in 1956, K4s #3750 has left the enginehouse and is proceeding east near ALAN tower which was built in 1934 to control the Camden terminal between the riverfront and Broadway station. Soon the 3750 will reverse and back against its train in the coach yard. This locomotive, built in 1920, was preserved for posterity by the PRR, and for a while masqueraded as the 1737, the first K4s, while stored in Northumberland. After it was relocated to the Railroad Museum of Pennsylvania at Strasburg, the Pacific regained its true identity.

(Below) Here is Train #135, enroute from its first station stop at 22 Federal Street to Broadway station. Rebuilt and greatly enlarged in 1952, Broadway took over from the old ferry terminal when that facility closed with the cessation of ferry service that year. However, there were still many commuters working at the various industries located along Delaware Avenue and also at the nearby PRSL and PRR Federal Street offices. To accommodate them, a few commuter runs, including Atlantic City Train #135, made a station stop at a remaining ferry terminal platform adjacent to the railroad offices; this practice was not indicated in timetables. No. 5439, one of the seventy-five K4-s built by Baldwin thirty years earlier, has only a few months left in this August 1957 scene.

(Both – Albert T. Holtz)

(Above) Inside the Camden Terminal Enginehouse, C T E as stenciled on locomotive pilots, PRR class AFP-20 #5753 is being serviced. This October 4, 1958, scene was recorded fifty-eight years after the twenty-stall roundhouse was constructed.

(Opposite page, top) Running light down Delaware Avenue from Coopers Point Yard toward Bulson Street Yard, is the 6000, resplendent in its new livery on March 24, 1968. The track passes the manufacturing facilities of Esterbrook Pen, RCA and Campbell Soup. After the arrival of the GP-38s, most remaining Baldwins gradually were painted in a similar scheme. The pilot stripes had first been applied about 1965, and even Pennsy Baldwins assigned to Camden got them. Apparently unique to this facility, the only previous Pennsy power with stripes were the center-cab transfer units and GE 44-tonners, and they were applied to the front end only.

Most southbound PRSL trains, both freight and passenger (aside from some outlying yard jobs) originated on the PRR. As may be seen from the accompanying map, Camden was truly a Pennsy town. But wherever you went along the PRR in Camden, you were bound to encounter PRSL trains or locomotives.

(Above – Frank C. Kozempel, opposite page, top – John P. Stroup)

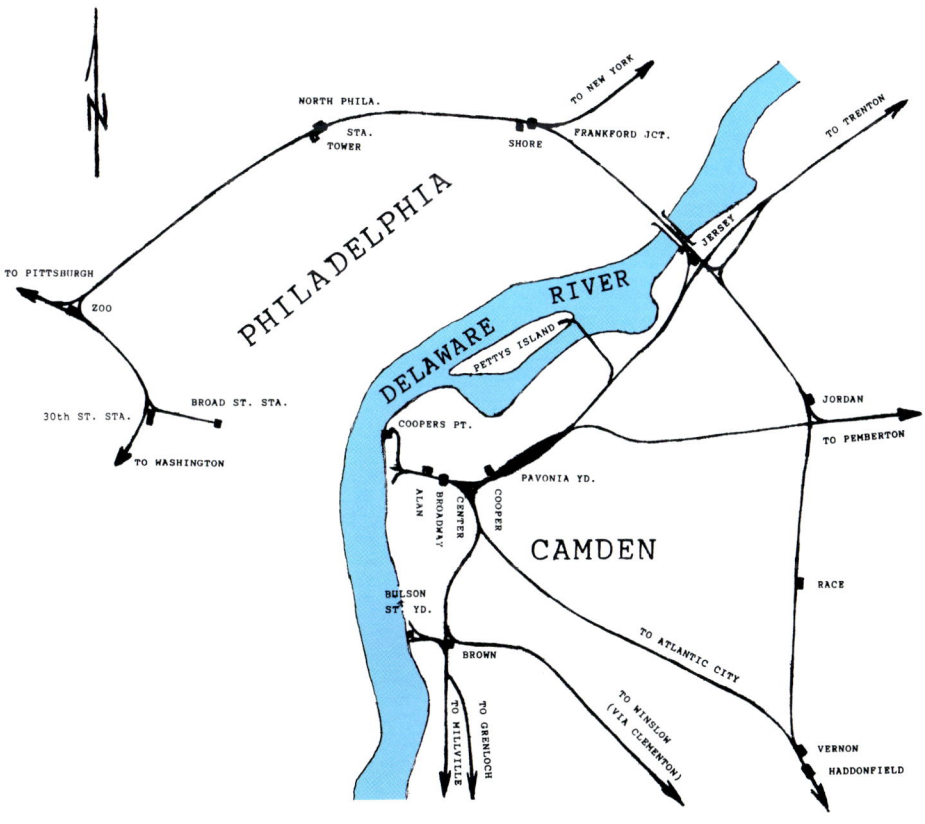

(Route map only, individual tracks not shown - JPS)

The PRSL's standard passenger cars, as well as the electric MU cars and three steel cabin cars, were all inherited from the West Jersey and Seashore. The PRSL started with 71 P-70 coaches, 21 PB-70 combines and 17 baggage-mail cars. By the 1940s these cars bore the following numbers:

Baggage – express	6428 – 6438
Coaches	9865 – 9936
Combines	9938 – 9962
Baggage – mail	9963 – 9966

As part of a New Jersey P U C service improvement order, a total of 40 P-70s were rebuilt during 1948 and 1949 by the PRR for PRSL service with air conditioning, new seats, luggage racks and lighting. Equipped with roller bearing trucks with integral brake cylinders, they were by far the best riding coaches to be regularly assigned to PRSL trains. Over the years, this fleet and the unrebuilt cars gradually diminished – most were scrapped, but a few were sold to other carriers, as occurred in 1961 when about 20 coaches were sold, reportedly to Mexico. One of these, #9922, is shown (above) in the Camden coach yard on October 28, 1961.

(Below) Baggage car #6437, probably the last PRSL one in use, is seen at Camden on November 19, 1960. During the last decade of locomotive-hauled trains, as the number of their serviceable cars declined, the PRSL gradually relied more heavily on the PRR. The Pennsy's own trains were shrinking, and it became increasingly common to see PRR coaches, as well as baggage cars, on PRSL's remaining Atlantic City trains.

(Both – John P. Stroup)

The Baldwin Diesel Locomotive and the PRSL

The Baldwin Locomotive Works, a Philadelphia corporation, constructed diesel locomotives at its huge facility in Eddystone, just south of Philadelphia. Baldwin switchers and road switchers arrived on the PRSL between 1950 and 1956 when the railroad was merely following the path of its two parents in purchasing Baldwins as needed for specific requirements. The Pennsy was acquiring what would become the largest fleet of Baldwin units owned by any carrier. However, the PRR had skipped over ordering the AS-16 (the PRSL's primary unit) for its big brother, the AS-616, distinguished by its six-wheel trucks with a total of six traction motors. Most of the Pennsy's eleven units worked in coal service in Ohio and West Virginia for much of their lives, although some migrated to the east in the 1960s. Two of them, the 8970 and 8971, built in 1951, were the only two of this model built with steam generators for any railroad. These two eventually were assigned to Camden in 1962, replacing the last two Alco PA-1 (AFP-20) units, #5757 and 5758. They were used on freight transfers and in local service both on the Pennsy and the PRSL, but not in passenger service, as their boilers were no doubt unserviceable.

The Reading meanwhile accumulated the most AS-16 units of any railroad, a total of 43, four with steam generators. The passenger units, #560 through 563, were built in 1951 and saw service on the PRSL in the summer from 1958 through the early 1960s. They were right at home, as the engine crews were obviously quite familiar with this power.

(Above) On July 21, 1960, Reading 560 is ready to depart the coach yard with two cars for the scheduled 4:26 p.m. departure from Broadway station as Train #769. Forty miles and an hour and twenty-two minutes later it will arrive in Millville. As the PRSL's own units were used to operate the Philadelphia trains, these Reading units were used on Camden-area trains during the summer when the normal RDCs instead operated additional service to Ocean City, Wildwood and Cape May.
(John P. Stroup)

(Above) The RDCs, the "second generation" of PRSL rail motor cars, were originally maintained at the old electric MU car repair shed, which was located on a Delaware River pier just south of the site of the ferry terminal. In February 1958 sparks from a welder's torch ignited the pier, and two RDCs, M404 and M412, along with the pier were destroyed. For several summers afterward, Budd Company loaned its demonstrator #2960 for use on the PRSL in exchange for an annual overhaul. After the fire, the cars were serviced adjacent to the roundhouse. Here M403 and M413 await their afternoon assignments on April 7, 1961.

(Below) Budd Company demonstrator #2960, built in July 1949, is seen at Camden on August 29, 1962, its shades drawn against the summer sun. As the PRSL's need for passenger equipment diminished, #2960 last saw use on the PRSL during the summer of 1964, and later was sold to the Canadian National to become their #6110.

(Opposite page, top) In this afternoon scene in September 1963, two PRSL commuter trains depart from the east end of the Pennsy's Broadway station in Camden. They will soon pass CENTER tower and head south onto home rails.

(Above and below – John P. Stroup, opposite page, top – Richard S. Short)

The PRSL utilized gas-electric rail motor cars on many of the lightly-trafficked rural branch lines. It had purchased two cars from the PRR in 1935 which were supplemented with Pennsy and Reading cars, similar to the practice regarding locomotive-hauled equipment. The two rail motor cars were retired in 1952 after the cessation of the service for which they had been acquired. The Budd RDCs M404 and M412 were destroyed by the Camden pier fire in 1958; the remainder of the RDCs were sold to NJDOT in 1969 and renumbered 5180 – 5189.

RAIL CAR ROSTER

Road Numbers	Builder	Class/Model	Serial Numbers	Built
400	Brill	OEW-250A	22385	7/26 as PRR 4635
401	Pullman/Brill	OEG-350B	6202 / 22697	4/29 as PRR 4654
M402 – M404	Budd	RDC-1	5101 – 5103	9/50
M405 – M407	Budd	RDC-1	5104 – 5106	10/50
M408 – M410	Budd	RDC-1	5307 – 5309	5/51
M411 – M413	Budd	RDC-1	5310, 5401, 5402	6/51

(Right) RDCs M413 and M410, running to Millville as Train #773, leave Camden's Twelfth Street Station at 5:44 p.m. and cross Federal Street on October 3, 1966. It is the first day of operation for this "terminal," which replaced Broadway when construction of the Patco Lindenwold High-Speed Line caused the PRSL to vacate its former station. Busses transferred passengers from the remaining SEPTA Bridge Speed Line station at Broadway to this location near Twelfth and Federal Streets. It was used for about five years until the Millville passenger service ended in 1971.
(John P. Stroup)

(Above) In this scene taken just west of the Route 30 overpass, train #CA-299 with the 6001 has pulled clear of the River Avenue crossing. In the distance, the Pennsy's Pemberton local, with engine #8975, is about to back west out of Twelfth Street Station and then come forward on the near track. This October 3, 1966, scene clearly illustrates the grade that westbounds had to contend with upon leaving Pavonia Yard.

Although this view was taken in 1966, it typified the motive power that was assigned to the Pennsy's Camden enginehouse during the previous ten years. As steam power was being phased out, numerous products of Baldwin were assigned in their places. By 1960 there were four 660 hp switchers, seven of 1000 hp, three of 1200 hp, two 1000 hp and one 1200 hp road switchers and one of the 2400 hp center-cab transfer units. Any of these units might be seen on the PRSL and engine crews would feel quite comfortable in handling these locomotives. Aside from the four GE 44-tonners and the two Alco PA-1 units still running in 1960, Camden was certainly a Baldwin haven. And don't forget the Reading road switchers in the summertime!

(Opposite page, top) It's September 30, 1966, and the River Avenue crossing watchman protects the passage of CA-289 departing for Atlantic City. The 6014 has backed its train past **COOPER**, and is now heading east around the south edge of Pavonia Yard to **HATCH** before proceeding south down the Bridge Branch to Haddonfield.

(Both – John P. Stroup)

PRR BALDWIN DIESELS ASSIGNED TO CAMDEN – 1960

Class	Road Numbers	Model	Serial Numbers	Built
BS-6	5941	VO-660	72821	10/45
BS-6a	9000, 9003, 9226	DS 4-4-660	73905, 73908, 73821	3/49, 3/49, 1/49
BS-10	5913, 5916, 5918	VO-1000	69662, 69665, 69784	9/43, 9/43, 11/43
BS-10a	5973, 9136, 9251, 9252	DS 4-4-1000	73591, 73765, 73864, 73865	3/48, 8/48, 12/48, 12/48
BS-10as	9276, 9277	DRS 4-4-1000	74403, 74404	2/49, 2/49
BS-12	8794	S-12	75309	2/52
BS-12as	8975	RS-12	75116	4/51
BS-12m	8767, 8768	S-12	75654, 75655	10/52, 10/52
BS-24	8953	RT-624	75124	8/51

8953 had C–C wheel arrangement, remainder were B–B

ARRANGED FREIGHT TRAIN SERVICE—SOUTHWARD
PENNSYLVANIA READING SEASHORE LINES
The time shown conveys no time-table authority.

Stations	WY-345 (2)	CA-299 (2)	WY-841 (2)	WY-843 (2)	WY-33 (2)	WY-27 (2)	WY-351 (2)	WY-51 (2)	WY-391 (2)	WY-79 (2)	WY-847 (3)	WY-343 (3)	CA-297 (2)	CM-91 (3)	CA-289 (3)
Leave	A.M.	A.M.	A.M.	A.M.	A.M.	A.M.	A.M.	A.M.	A.M.	A.M.	P.M.	P.M.	P.M.	P.M.	P.M.
PAVONIA YD.		6.40	6.45	7.45	8.20	8.45		9.45		10.45	12.30		9.00	10.00	10.45
BULSON ST. YD.															
GIBBSTOWN											1.30				
CARNEY'S PT.				3.00											
DEEP WATER POINT			10.30												
SALEM									3.00						
WILLIAMSTOWN						3.00									
BRIDGETON										2.30					
CLAYTON	12.01														
MILLVILLE	5.30				11.30		8.55					7.30			
LEESBURG							1.15								
PASSERELLI SDG.												11.30			
CAPE MAY CT. HSE.										10.30					
CAPE MAY										1.00				3.30	
WILLIAMSTOWN JCT.		11.30													
HAMMONTON														1.00	
ATLANTIC CITY															1.45
Arrive	A.M.	A.M.	A.M.	P.M.	A.M.	P.M.	P.M.	P.M.	P.M.	P.M.	P.M.	P.M.	A.M.	A.M.	A.M.

(1) Sunday only. (2) Daily except Sunday. (3) Daily except Saturday.

The influence and assistance of "parents" Pennsylvania Railroad and Reading Company could be readily seen on the PRSL.

(Above) This PRSL inspection train is enroute from Philadelphia to Atlantic City via Camden. Freshly-painted #6024 leads Reading office car #15 and Pennsy #7504, the *William Penn,* across the Cooper River on May 1, 1963.

CAMDEN COUNTY PORTION OF PRR'S BORDENTOWN BRANCH

Interlocking	Interlocking Station	Block Station	Block-Limit Station	STATIONS	Dist. from Camden	Sidings Assign. direc'n Car capacity 50 ft. cars		
						West	East	Both
				CAMDEN				
X	X			ALAN	0.4			
				BROADWAY	0.6			
X	X	X		CENTER	1.0			
				COOPER	1.5			
				PAVONIA	2.5			
				HATCH				
X	X	X		JERSEY	4.8			
				DISTRICT POST (Phila. District)	4.9			
				DELAIR	5.0			
				MINSON	5.7			

(Opposite page, top) The PRSL had access to Pennsy locomotives, both in steam and diesel eras, as the maintenance of PRSL power was at the Pennsy's engine facilities in Camden. Being a two-way arrangement, it was not unusual to see PRSL diesels on the PRR Bordentown and Pemberton Branches. Although it was a Pennsy enginehouse, there were more PRSL locomotives serviced at Camden than the PRR had assigned here for maintenance. Some PRR power that appeared on the PRSL, such as these EFS-17m (EMD GP-9) units, were not even assigned to Camden, but had merely brought a transfer run into Pavonia from Morrisville or South Philadelphia. These units, #7188 and 7044, with PRSL cabin car #234, roll over the same bridge as shown above on September 30, 1966, enroute to pick up their train at Bulson Street Yard. While heavy trains crossed this bridge, they had to make a "run for the hill " due to a rapid change in elevation, as the railroad ascends a short but steep grade to cross over Route 30 and Federal Street before reaching CENTER tower. This embankment tied in with a similar one from west of Broadway station constructed by the PRR in 1907 in a grade crossing elimination project. At CENTER tower, about midway on the embankment, PRSL trains from either direction would head south to gain home rails.

(Both – John P. Stroup)

ARRANGED FREIGHT TRAIN SERVICE—NORTHWARD
PENNSYLVANIA READING SEASHORE LINES
The time shown conveys no time-table authority.

Stations	CM-90 (2)	WY-344 (2)	CA-290 (4)	WY-390 (2)	WY-350 (2)	WY-34 (2)	CA-300 (2)	WY-846 (3)	WY-840 (2)	WY-842 (2)	WY-50 (2)	WY-26 (2)	WY-80 (2)	CA-298 (3)	WY-346 (3)
Arrive	A.M.	A.M.	A.M.	A.M.	P.M.	P.M.	P.M.	P.M.	P.M.	P.M.	P.M.	P.M.	P.M.	P.M.	P.M.
PAVONIA YD.	3.00		5.30			4.30	5.00	6.00	6.30	7.00	7.20	7.40	8.00	8.45	
BULSON ST. YD.															
GIBBSTOWN								3.00							
CARNEY'S PT.										4.00					
DEEP WATER POINT									1.30						
SALEM											3.30				
WILLIAMSTOWN												3.30			
BRIDGETON													3.00		
CLAYTON															
MILLVILLE		3.30			4.00	1.30									11.30
LEESBURG					1.30										9.45
PASSERELLI SDG.		12.01													
CAPE MAY CT. HSE.				10.00											
CAPE MAY	7.30			8.00											
WILLIAMSTOWN JCT.							1.30								
HAMMONTON			2.00												
ATLANTIC CITY														5.45	
Leave	P.M.	A.M.	A.M.	A.M.	P.M.	P.M.	P.M.	P.M.	P.M.	P.M.	P.M.	P.M.	P.M.	P.M.	P.M.

(1) Sunday only. (2) Daily except Sunday. (3) Daily except Saturday. (4) Daily except Monday.

(Right) As a tenant in PRR's Pavonia Yard, the PRSL accounted for most of the departures and arrivals at the west end of the yard. **COOPER** tower controlled this flow, and the River Avenue crossing provided a great vantage point for the passing parade. On December 29, 1961, WY-841, bound for the Penns Grove Branch, is leaving behind the 6023, a frequent assignment for this unit and sister 6022.

The PRSL's final six Baldwin road switchers, #6022 through 6027, were originally built for the Reading Company as part of a ten-unit order in 1953. As production was nearing completion, the Reading canceled the final six. Baldwin finally found a buyer in 1955 as the PRSL needed more units to eliminate steam power from its off-season operations. These six engines had been built to a new design with enlarged hoods to accommodate options that various customers could order, such as steam generators and dynamic brakes. In fact, these units had contained dynamic brakes and different control stands, both of which were removed prior to the sale to the PRSL. The 6022 and 6023 were not steam generator equipped, were a little lighter in weight and were geared for freight service. The 6024 through 6027 were seen at the head end of PRSL passenger trains through 1969, after which these and the other BS-16ms units continued lugging PRSL freight trains until one by one they were retired. Three of them, 6016, 6024 and 6025, were still active when Conrail took over in April 1976, and at least the 6024 was used in switching service until August before all three were retired in October of that year. New Conrail numbers in the 8300 series had been assigned to all remaining Baldwins, but none were ever applied.

(Below) Also on December 29, 1961, shortly after WY-841 has passed WY-79 accelerates past **COOPER** enroute to Bridgeton with Pennsy class AFP-20 #5758, an Alco PA-1, as power. This unit and sister 5757 were frequently used on this train at this time as they had less than a year left in service and were literally running their last miles. As the Bridgeton Branch had light rail on a cinder roadbed and by this time was not very well maintained, the use of this type of power, which spread the locomotive weight over six axles, was actually an advantage over a four-axle unit. Of course, the crews were not fond of switching industries or worse yet running backward for any distance with this former mainline hauler.

(Both – John P. Stroup)

As more and more reconstruction around Camden developed due to the Patco Lindenwold High-Speed Line, Pavonia Yard underwent major alteration and the classic wooden **COOPER** tower was razed to make way for lead tracks to the new Pavonia enginehouse. In its place, across River Avenue, a new concrete block **COOPER** was constructed, primarily to control the passage of the PRSL jobs. Originally, neither "**COOPER**" tower controlled the River Avenue crossing, but was protected by a watchman, as most of the rail action near the crossing consisted of slow back and forth moves, many of which didn't actually reach the road. However, by the time of these 1972 scenes, gates had been installed, and the operator at **COOPER** assumed the duty of activating them in advance of through movements.

(Above) On April 23, 1972, CA-299 leaves the yard in a cloud of exhaust behind the 2001. Since all of the PRSL's GP-38s were equipped with dual control stands, sights such as this long-hood-forward operation were quite common.

(Below) Six days later, yard runner #22-A with a transfer to Bulson Street Yard, is using the 6030 and 6032 in MU. Although the last group of switchers were equipped for multiple unit operation, this was rarely the practice on the PRSL.

(Both – John P. Stroup)

CLEMENTON BRANCH

At **BROWN** tower in South Camden, the Clementon Branch strikes out southeasterly toward its eventual rendezvous with the Atlantic City mainline and the Cape May Branch at Winslow. In between, it passes through a host of towns that manage to provide enough business for two daily local freights, and also act as a conduit for through traffic to mainline and Cape May County points as well as some Jersey Central interchange business. This portion of the Atlantic City Railroad was first constructed as a narrow-gauge line in 1877; the Reading standard-gauged and substantially upgraded the line in 1884.

(Above) Train #CA-297 receives train orders at **BROWN** on its way to Williamstown Junction. Today, February 1, 1970, there are seventy-seven cars behind the 2003 and 2009. With its growing need for additional power, the PRSL ordered a third group of five GP-38s from EMD for mid-1970 delivery. Unfortunately, the Penn Central bankruptcy in June of that year caused financing to be withdrawn, and the railroad struggled on with its existing power until the Conrail startup in 1976. The five GP-38s ended up on Penn Central later in 1970, retaining their 2010 - 2014 numbering, and ironically were assigned to Camden's Pavonia enginehouse, as if to tease the PRSL. They were used singly on local PC runs but were not borrowed for PRSL trains.

(John P. Stroup)

CLEMENTON BRANCH

Interlocking	Interlocking Station	Block Station	Block-Limit Station	STATIONS	Dist. from Camden	Sidings Assign. direc'n Car capacity 50 ft. cars		
						North	South	Both
X	X	X		BROWN	2.8			
				SHIPYARD	3.0			
				WEST COLLINGSWOOD	4.5			
				OAKLYN	5.1			
				AUDUBON	5.8			
				ORSTON	6.3			
				HADDON HEIGHTS	6.9			21
				BARRINGTON	7.6			
				MAGNOLIA	9.2			
				SOMERDALE	10.3			
				STRATFORD	11.3			
				LAUREL SPRINGS	12.0			
				GARDEN LAKE	12.5			
				CLEMENTON	13.4			12
				PINE VALLEY	14.8			
				ALBION	16.0			
				PENBRYN	17.4			
				WILLIAMSTOWN JCT.	18.2			85
				FLORENCE	19.7			
				CEDAR BROOK	21.3			
				BRADDOCK	22.4			
				BLUE ANCHOR	23.3			
X	X	X		WINSLOW	25.9			

X—indicates in service continuously.

In 1962 the Reading Company discontinued its car-float operation on the Delaware River between Port Richmond and two locations in Camden, the primary one being Bulson Street Yard. Not only was the marine service increasingly expensive to operate, but the Reading had contracted with Atlantic City Electric Company to provide coal for its new Beesley's Point generating station. Thus the Reading had no choice but to work out an agreement with the Pennsy to provide the route from Philadelphia to **CENTER** tower in Camden and then on to Bulson Street Yard.

(Above) A Beesley's Point Extra behind half of the PRSL's "high hoods," #6022-6023-6027, accelerates through Oaklyn on November 24, 1968, after picking up additional cars at West Collingswood. In an odd coincidence, these three units were all retired at the same time in 1971.

(Below) After leaving the city of Camden, the string of suburban towns of West Collingswood, Oaklyn, Audubon, Haddon Heights, Barrington, Magnolia, Somerdale, Stratford and Laurel Springs extend to Clementon, a little over ten miles south of **BROWN** tower. CA-299 is entering Haddon Heights behind the 6017 on May 10, 1969, having just passed through Audubon. In 1953 the PRSL purchased five Baldwin model S-12 switchers, 6017 – 6021. These units were part of the continuing program to purge steam power from the railroad and were utilized in all but express passenger service. They remained an intergral part of the roster until the absorption of the PRSL into Conrail.

(Both – William M. Tilden)

HADDON HEIGHTS

(Above) Constructed in 1890, the stations in West Collingswood, Audubon and Haddon Heights were nearly identical. Surviving into the Conrail era, the Audubon and Haddon Heights stations have managed to celebrate their one-hundredth birthday. The lights are glowing warmly inside and out at the Haddon Heights station on this gloomy January 10, 1968.

The area from Oaklyn through Haddon Heights provided excellent surroundings for railroad photography, as illustrated by these scenes of CA-299 at Haddon Heights.

(Opposite page, top) On July 1, 1970, the 6016 brings its train past the station. This was generally the first stop for this local freight, and once clear of the crossing, the train would ease to a halt.

(Opposite page, bottom) In March 1973, engine 2007 heads south with the local on a crystal clear day. CA-299 has been depicted with the PRSL's three types of power: Baldwin switchers, Baldwin road switchers and EMD GP-38's. This indicates the wide range of service these units could handle, as the railroad rarely kept certain power on particular runs.

(Above – Robert L. Long, opposite page, top – John P. Stroup, opposite page, bottom – William J. Coxey)

85

(Opposite page, top) In a 1971 experiment to increase visibility to motorists at grade crossings, two GP-38s, #2003 and 2008, received silver pilots, trucks and fuel tanks. While at first they were brighter, road grime quickly tarnished their appearance, and a return to black soon followed. Here the 2003 is leaving Haddon Heights with CA-299 on October 11, 1971.

(Opposite page, bottom) Almost in the same spot, but seen from the overhead I-295 embankment, is CA-299 once again, this time with the 6001 as power on the late fall day of November 7, 1966. Although fifteen years old now, the PRSL's original diesels could still lug a good-sized train.

(Below) The next town is the pleasant suburb of Barrington, site of an Owens-Corning fiberglass insulation plant. Various communities along the railroad helped keep the right-of-way from becoming an eyesore by establishing beautification programs, such as this small area in Barrington. The 6021 is entering town with CA-299 on August 24, 1971.

(All – John P. Stroup)

BARRINGTON

(Above) Near the south end of Barrington on April 27, 1969, GP-38 #2000 is rolling CA-297 past the searchlight signals. It is small details such as signals, the rail (a unique Reading style rolled in the mid-1920s) or even the style of a telephone pole line that distinguished one branch from another, even on a small road such as the PRSL. The signals shown were installed in 1940 to replace the original Reading Hall-type model.

(Below) Three Reading units power a Beesley's Point train between the signals at Barrington on February 22, 1970. After having their train assembled at Port Richmond, the 469-515-2751, two RS-3s and an SW-1500, had brought the seventy cars into Camden earlier in the day. Occasionally, when PRSL power was unavailable, the train was recrewed at South Camden and run intact to the power plant.

(Above – William M. Tilden, below – John P. Stroup)

MAGNOLIA

LAUREL SPRINGS

(Above) CA-299 is rolling into Magnolia with thirty-five cars in tow behind borrowed PRR BS-12 #8796, in another example of the PRSL's use of Pennsy's Camden power; this is March 28, 1955, and the PRSL's final batch of its own switchers, 6028 through 6033, won't be delivered for another year. Two sister units to the 8796, the 8794 and 8795, were also assigned to Camden, but by 1960 only the 8794 remained.

(Below) Train #609 pulls away from its 6:10 p.m. Laurel Springs station stop, almost at the end of its run to Clementon, on a September day in 1963. After the one roundtrip commuter service had been cut back from Hammonton to Clementon in 1961, the lightly patronized train was discontinued altogether in 1965. Laurel Springs was officially incorporated in 1893, although the poet Walt Whitman had frequented the town over the years prior to his death in 1892. About a mile and a half south of Laurel Springs is Clementon, once noted for its lake and huge amusement park that had been started by a local trolley company. Below there, the country was mostly rural, with the gradual increase of pine lands, punctuated with an occasional small town en route to Winslow.

(Above – Frank C. Kozempel, below – Robert L. Long)

WILLIAMSTOWN JCT.

Five miles past Clementon, Williamstown Junction is no longer a "junction." Prior to the original construction of the Clementon route a line had been built west from Atco, where a connection existed with a Jersey Central branch from their Southern Division mainline. It was built by another Reading predecessor through Williamstown to Glassboro and on to Mullica Hill. The Clementon route crossed this Atco line east of Williamstown at what became known as Williamstown Junction. When the PRSL was formed the section between Williamstown and Williamstown Junction was abandoned in 1934, and the portion to Atco was removed in 1942. However, the name "Williamstown Junction" remained through the years.

(Above) Dusk is settling in on January 12, 1968. The sidings to the south of the station are quiet as train CA-296 has finished its work and is headed back to Pavonia.

(Left) Two years later, on February 22, 1970, engine #2004 is working train CA-296 after the passage of a Beesley's Point extra powered by Reading units. The local will shortly depart Williamstown Junction for Camden and the activity for the day will cease once again.

(Above – Robert L. Long, left – John P. Stroup)

(Above) Adjacent to Williamstown Junction is the site of a G.F. Pettinos sand pit. Here, on December 27, 1954, two year old PRR ES-12m (EMD SW-9) #8524 is drilling the sand pit spur. During the early 1950s EMD model GP-7 and SW-9 power were frequently used out of Camden on various PRR locals and occasionally on the PRSL, such as this assignment to train CA-299. This was due to the gradual phase-out of steam concurrent with the arrival of diesel replacements. Until a sufficient number of Baldwins were assigned to Camden, EMD and similar Alco power was also used. Several EMD SW-9s, including the 8524, were assigned to the Meadows enginehouse in northern New Jersey and operated in pairs on train #A-5 to Pavonia. While laying over at Camden between runs they were used locally until that train was discontinued in the early 1960s.

(Below) The only steam-powered fan trip to operate on the PRSL after regular steam operations ended ran from Camden to Cape May and return on Sunday, May 5, 1968. This high-speed excursion used Steamtown #127, a former Canadian Pacific light 4-6-2 to power the High Iron Co. trip. Here, the fifteen car train barrels through Winslow on the Clementon Branch, just north of the junction to Cape May.

(Above – Frank C. Kozempel, below – John P. Stroup)

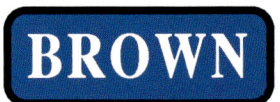

Constructed to help facilitate the consolidation of former PRR and Reading operations at the Camden end of the PRSL, **BROWN** lies at the junction of the Clementon and Millville Branches. Prior to the merger, the lines crossed just south of this site, where the Reading mainline from Kaighn's Point ferry terminal and Bulson Street Yard extended to the seashore via Clementon.

(Above) Backing into Bulson Street Yard, PRR B-6sb #4183 is working yard runner 22-A on July 20, 1954. The Camden Brewery in the background was at one time a major customer of the PRSL, both for inbound ingredients and outbound beer.

(Below) As seen from the tower, Salem bound WY-51 has the 8686, a PRR class H-10s with eighteen cars on May 18, 1955. The Salem freight was primarily an agricultural hauler, with a large portion of its returning loads destined for Campbell Soup Co. in Camden in addition to finished products from packing and canning companies.

(Both – Frank C. Kozempel)

(Above) This is 22-A once again, this time utilizing sister B-6sb #4182 on April 22, 1955. The industrial nature of this area serves as a backdrop for these scenes. The Langston Company's corrugated cardboard box machinery factory dominates the neighborhood.

(Right) A short while later, another yard runner, the 23-A, is coming off the Clementon Branch with the 557, another class B-6sb, with eleven cars. Although a southerly wind is blowing the exhaust ahead of the engine, the train is actually headed north. The B-6sb class engines featured here were all PRR locomotives, but the PRSL also had five of their own, albeit former Pennsy power, via the West Jersey and Seashore. One of them, the 6095, was the last PRSL steam locomotive in use, finally succumbing in 1952. All of the PRSL's fleet of steam locomotives was inherited from the West Jersey and Seashore, none coming from the Reading. The locomotives were of three wheel arrangements, 0-6-0, 2-8-0 and 4-4-2, and representatives of each survived into the early 1950s. However, both PRR and Reading steam continued to be used by the PRSL, particularly during the busy summer season.
(Both – Frank C. Kozempel)

In the diesel era now, a variety of power is seen at **BROWN**. This area was usually busy, with transfer runs, the yard jobs at nearby Bulson Street Yard and trains for various branches.

(Above) A still bright and clean 6006, the PRSL's first diesel switcher, has yard runner 23-A in hand on August 7, 1954. In 1950, Baldwin switcher production incorporated just two models as design changes introduced the S-8 and S-12. The PRSL sampled the S-8 in 1951 with #6006, but when more switchers were ordered in 1953 they were of the more powerful S-12 model.

(Opposite page, top) A Beesley's Point Extra waits for the signal after backing its eighty-four cars north from the "middle" track. The 2006-2005-2002 are ready to go on February 1, 1970. During the winter months in the early 1970s engines 2005 and 2006 sported yellow snow plows.

(Opposite page, bottom) WY-841 is leaving town on August 6, 1965, behind PRR AS-16ms (Alco RS-3) #8472. This unit had been assigned previously to the Pittsburgh area for commuter service. Although not actually assigned to Camden, the 8472 was used on local freights during this month, including several PRSL runs. The Alco model RS-3 was the equivalent of the PRSL's Baldwin model AS-16 units. Many Pennsy RS-3s contained the same options that the PRSL chose for their Baldwins. The 8472 was a particularly good match, as it was equipped with multiple-unit, a steam generator and dual control stands.
(Above – Frank C. Kozempel, opposite page, both – John P. Stroup)

(Above) Bulson Street Yard, once part of the Reading's Camden terminal complex, is quite active on this day in March 1968. The Reading coal train from Port Richmond has arrived, the yard job is busy and two local freights are making pick-ups.

(Below) The float bridges are seen from the Delaware River in September 1966. After the Reading acquired trackage rights over the Pennsy's Delair Bridge in April 1962, these float bridges were abandoned, but Bulson Street Yard remained an important facility for the PRSL. As the Reading Company's traffic continued to be interchanged here many trains that originated at Pavonia made pick-ups at Bulson Street before continuing south. The Reading coal for Beesley's Point usually was yarded here before making its journey to the power plant.

(Both – Robert L. Long)

The Beesley's Point coal was brought over from Port Richmond most often behind three Reading RS-3s. On the other hand, the general freights to Bulson Street usually had two units. On occasion, a set of Baldwin switchers rebuilt with EMD prime movers would show up, as would some EMD SW-1500s. Mixtures of these units also occurred. In early 1965 the Reading even used pairs of their own Baldwin AS-16s a few times.

(Above) Looking south from **BROWN** tower, BR-2 has backed out of Bulson Street Yard on its return run to Philadelphia in October 1967 behind the 482 and 498. Looming in the background is the huge New York Shipbuilding Co. complex, at one time one of Camden's largest employers and a significant railroad customer.

(Below) An unusual use of four RS-3s (492-486-499-512) is depicted on February 10, 1968, as RB-1 works its train beneath the Broadway overpass at the entrance to Bulson Street Yard. Cold weather had an adverse effect on the ability of railroad equipment to move easily, and most likely this condition prompted the use of additional power.

(Above – William J. Coxey, below – Joseph J. Grella)

MILLVILLE BRANCH
MANUMUSKIN AND LEESBURG SECONDARY TRACK

Interlocking	Interlocking Station	Block Station	Block-Limit Station	STATIONS	Dist. from Camden	Sidings Assign. direc'n Car capacity 50 ft. cars		
						North	South	Both
X	X			CAMDEN				
				ALAN	0.4			
				BROADWAY	0.6			
X	X	X		CENTER	1.0			
				DISTRICT POST (Atl. Dist.)	1.03			
				SOUTH CAMDEN	2.5			
X	X	X		BROWN	2.8			
				YORKSHIP	3.0			
				GLOUCESTER	4.3			
				SOUTH GLOUCESTER	4.9			
				BROOKLAWN	5.5		19	
				WESTVILLE	6.1			
				SOUTH WESTVILLE	6.7		33	
				NORTH WOODBURY	7.9			
B	B	B		WOODBURY	8.8			45
				WOODBURY HEIGHTS	10.2			
				WENONAH	11.9			
				SEWELL	13.7			
				PITMAN	16.3			
B	B	B		GLASSBORO	18.2			
				SOUTH GLASSBORO	19.0			
			X	CLAYTON	21.9			
				FRANKLINVILLE	24.6			75
				IONA	25.7			
				MALAGA	28.2			
		B	B	LAKE	29.5			
		B	B	NEWFIELD	30.4			
				NORTH VINELAND	31.8			
			X	HOME	34.0			43
				LANDIS	34.5			
				VINELAND	34.6			
			X	SOUTH VINELAND	37.4			53
				MILLVILLE	40.0			12
		B		SWIFT	40.2			
			X	WOOD	41.2			
			X	WOOD	41.2			
				MENANTICO	43.6			
			X	MANUMUSKIN	46.8			
				TERMINUS	48.5			
				MANUMUSKIN	46.8			
				PORT ELIZABETH	48.6			
				MAURICETOWN	50.2			
				DORCHESTER	51.4			
				LEESBURG—880 ft. South of	52.5			

(Stations from WOOD through TERMINUS are on the MANUMUSKIN SEC. TRACK; stations from MANUMUSKIN through LEESBURG are on the LEESBURG SEC. TRACK.)

X—indicates in service continuously.
B—indicates in service part time.

(Above) Crossing the tidal marshes of Newton Creek on July 17, 1970, Train #769 barely disturbs fishermen on both banks as it heads toward Glassboro at 4:35 p.m. Later, Budd car M413 will return to Camden as non-revenue Train #770 and then run to Millville as Train #773. These moves were interspersed between various freight trains making their return trips to Pavonia Yard. This rather rural scene in South Camden is quite a contrast to what is behind the photographer, the huge complex of New York Shipbuilding Company which straddles Newton Creek at its confluence with the Delaware River.

(John P. Stroup)

(Above) Appearing to be a train heading toward Millville, this is really a Beesley's Point Extra that has made a double by pulling cars from the "middle" track south of **BROWN** and is well south of the Walt Whitman Bridge in Gloucester City. As soon as the train clears the switch, it will stop and then back past **BROWN** and up the grade in order to clear the interlocking. Once given the signal at **BROWN**, the train will proceed down the Clementon Branch. For this one-hundred and twelve car train on April 27, 1969, the railroad has assigned 2004-2009-2007-2002, a practice usually reserved for trains in excess of ninety cars. This eliminated the need to provide a pusher engine, as there were grades at Audubon and Albion on the Clementon Branch.

(John P. Stroup)

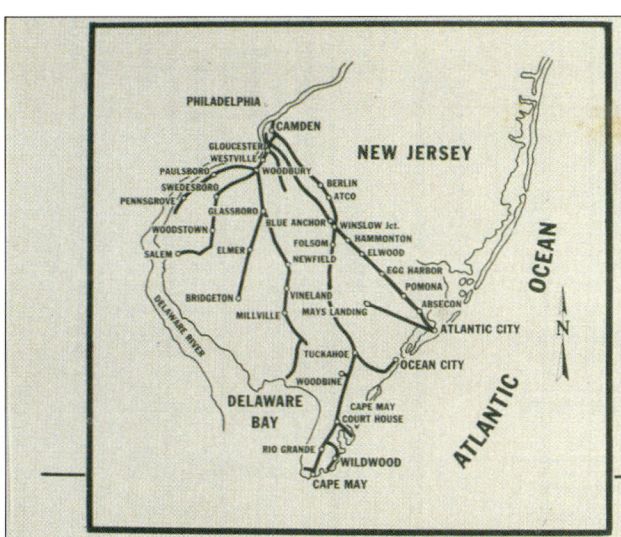

SOUTHERN NEW JERSEY is on the verge of a great industrial invasion. Opportunity exists in most towns served by Pennsylvania-Reading Seashore Lines to establish your new plant in healthy, comfortable surroundings close to popular seashore vacation and recreational resorts.

In your future planning, you would do well to investigate this area before making your final decision on plant location.

Southern New Jersey is a wonderful place to work—to live—to play.

PENNSYLVANIA-READING SEASHORE LINES

GLOUCESTER

A mile and a half south of **BROWN** tower is the city of Gloucester, still in Camden County. Noted for years as a manufacturing community, this blue-collar town is located between the Delaware River and a busy PRSL branch and was the first major stop of the Millville commuter trains. The one-time extensive Railway Post Office service from Camden was gradually reduced, until in the post-war years only the seashore area and Cumberland County routes remained. In 1946 Cape May lost its service, with Bridgeton, Wildwood and Atlantic City eliminated in 1949. This left the last PRSL R.P.O. line, known as the "Phila. & Millville," which served Gloucester, and succumbed in 1952.

(Above) WY-33 is en route to Millville on the morning of September 7, 1968, with the 2004 and 2000 on the point. The double-track had been retained as far as North Woodbury and both tracks were used for running in either direction. Three short portions of the center express track from the electric MU days were retained also.

(Right) During the last year of Millville passenger service the lone Budd Car is seen returning to Camden from its run as Train #769 to Glassboro, and will later make its run as Train #773 to Millville on this day in October 1970. This procedure was established for the final year and a half of service.

BROOKLAWN

(Opposite page, both) Another mile downline is Brooklawn, where train #WY-847 is heading south behind the 6004 and 6000 on December 23, 1967. While crossing the Little Timber Creek the train meets northbound train WY-34 and their cabin cars pass on the bridge.

(Above – John P. Stroup, below – Ronald H. Baile, opposite page, both – John P. Stroup)

WESTVILLE

Just south of Brooklawn is Westville, location of a huge Texaco refinery. Westville became the site of a major electric generating plant in 1906, but not the kind that first comes to mind. This was a railroad-owned power plant, to generate electricity for third-rail passenger train service. In 1905 the Pennsy had decided to electrify its suburban service to Millville and at the same time provide frequent and less expensive service to Atlantic City. The demand for travel to the shore was pushing the capacity of the main line to the limit, while the longer and underutilized route via Newfield could become the needed safety valve. The sixty-five mile route between Camden and Atlantic City was electrified with 600 volt d.c., but initially the ten miles between Newfield and Millville had overhead trolley wire, as did the 2.5 mile stretch between Camden and the south end of Gloucester City. The Millville section was converted to third-rail in 1910, but the northern portion remained under wire until the end, due primarily to concern for public safety at the numerous grade crossings. In addition to the Westville generators, there were eight sub-stations to distribute power to the line.

Rolling stock was constructed by three car builders in 1906 and consisted of: 62 MP-1 coaches, 2 MO-1 combines, 2 baggage-mail cars and 2 baggage-express cars, all of wooden construction. In 1909, 18 more coaches of class MP-2 were added. These cars differed in that they were equipped with steel ends. The last cars were of all-steel construction built in 1912 and consisted of 15 class MP-54 coaches and 2 class MPB-54 combines.

(Above) In this post-war scene, steel-ended car #6763 and two mates grind to a halt at the Westville station, just south of the powerhouse.

(Collectibles from Bob's Photos)

In 1924 the Pennsy decided to utilize a lower-cost outside source of power and contracted with Philadelphia Electric Company, which installed a high tension line from its Somerset Generating Station in Philadelphia to Westville. The steel towers which carried the line were installed along the west side of the Bridge Branch to Haddonfield and then followed a railroad-owned right-of-way to Westville. This portion of the route was originally acquired to carry a never-constructed bypass around Camden between Westville and a planned freight yard along the Bridge Branch in Pennsauken.

As the 1920s were drawing to a close, the Pennsy's grip on public transportation to Atlantic City was weakening, and electric service between Newfield and Atlantic City was withdrawn in 1931. By 1948 the railroad was operating the Millville MU service with 26 wooden cars and 15 steel ones. As accidents with the antiquated wooden cars had contributed to many fatalities nationwide, the State of New Jersey mandated that all such conveyances be removed from revenue service by year-end 1948. As the 15 steel cars were not enough to maintain the Millville schedule, at first the railroad cut back MU service to Glassboro. However, because of the high cost of this limited electric operation, the PRSL replaced the MU service with steam-powered trains between Camden and Millville in 1949. After delivery of the Baldwin road switchers the next year, many of the runs were dieselized; the subsequent delivery of the Budd RDCs soon provided the primary equipment for this line until the end of service in 1971.

(Below) The Public Service Electric Company's electric transmission overbuild dominates this Westville view, taken in almost the same spot as the electric MU scene. The transmission line is not railroad-related, although the supports do resemble catenary structures. RDC #M403, running as Train #769, is southbound, while runner 23-A waits on the middle siding with engine 6031 as power at 4:42 p.m. on April 16, 1965.

(John P. Stroup)

PRSL ELECTRIC CAR ROSTER

Road Numbers	Type
5135, 5136	Wooden Combine
5137, 5138	Steel Combine
5457, 5458	Wooden Bag.–Mail
6422, 6423	Wooden Bag.–Exp.
6700 – 6779	Wooden Coach
6780 – 6794	Steel Coach

WOODBURY

GLASSBORO

The county seat of Gloucester County, Woodbury is nearly three miles south of Westville and was known at one time for its glass manufacturing. The West Jersey Railroad arrived in Woodbury in 1857 as the town prospered significantly.

(Above) Late in the day on May 27, 1969, engine 2006 makes a set out at Woodbury. South of the city, the communities of Wenonah, Sewell and Pitman are passed before reaching Glassboro, another town once known for glass production. It was home to several carload producing industries, the largest being an Owens-Corning bottle cap plant.

(Below) At Glassboro, the operator is retrieving his order hoops as WY-33 rumbles past with thirty-four cars trailing the 6005 and 6004 on February 25, 1955. This daily except Sunday freight made few stops en route to Millville, and usually could make a quick return to Camden.

The six units of class BS-15ms were originally purchased in 1950 for the purpose of dieselizing the Millville commuter line. Pressure had been applied by the State of New Jersey's Public Utility Commission to improve service in response to complaints from the public. Units 6000 through 6005 were freed from their original passenger assignment when the Budd RDCs were acquired in 1951. In addition to the steam generator option, the PRSL had wisely ordered the diesels equipped with multiple-unit control and they quickly proved their worth lugging freight.

(Above – William M. Tilden, below – Frank C. Kozempel)

Glassboro achieved world recognition on June 23 and 25, 1967, when U.S. President Johnson met here with Soviet Premier Kosygin. The "summit" meeting was held to discuss mutual concerns on world issues including problems in the Middle East, nuclear proliferation and the Vietnam war. The site of the meeting was Glassboro State College, the presence of which greatly contributed to the charm of this town.

(Above) However, as shown in November of that year, the same could not be said of the railroad's appearance, certainly not conducive to patronage. An RDC has just stopped at the station en route to Millville; in the distance, WY-34 is making its way north to Camden.

(Below) Nearly four miles south of Glassboro, the next stop was Clayton. The station scene in May 1964 shows how rural the area was just twenty-two miles from Camden.

Franklinville was next, and although not important to the PRSL, it had a place in railroad history. After completion of the West Jersey and Seashore third-rail electrification, the Pennsy was busy at work on another electrification project that would put this one to the test. The New York Penn Station and tunnel operation would require electric locomotives, initially just to Manhattan Transfer near Newark. In order to determine the best possible type of locomotive, three prototypes were constructed, #10001, 10002 and 10003. In 1907 they were extensively tested at Franklinville, along with New Haven EP-1 #028, and eventually the features of the 10003 were settled upon. Sixty-six locomotives (thirty-three paired units) were constructed of class DD-1, entering service in 1910. The testing had paid off, as some of these locomotives lasted in non-revenue service until 1969! Thus Franklinville's contribution to railroad technology. *(Both – Robert L. Long)*

NEWFIELD

Newfield, six miles south of Franklinville, is the last town before Vineland and the junction of the former electric line to Atlantic City. On the night of August 19, 1954, an extra freight from Atlantic City with engine 6016 was proceeding into Newfield. As it got to the switch leading to the north leg of the wye, the 6016 split the switch and with three cars went on the ground.

(Above) PRR 120-ton wrecker #490704 is shown the next day cleaning up the mess.

(Below) Power for the wreck train from Camden is K4s #5495, standing by to assist when needed, not exactly its usual type of work on the head end of passenger expresses.

(Opposite page, top) Train WY-27 is arriving at Newfield with #6000 in charge of three cars on December 3, 1953. It is shown taking the north leg of the wye to the Newfield Branch, formerly the electric line to Atlantic City. Engine #6000 is right at home here, as the 1950 purchase of the BS-15ms units was done with the Millville Branch in mind.

(Opposite page, bottom) Here, fireman William Lafferty is spotting a car as WY-27 works around Newfield, before heading off to Mays Landing. The through trackage to Atlantic City would be severed in 1959 when the portion from here to Mays Landing was abandoned.

(All – Frank C. Kozempel)

VINELAND

In 1861, the year after the railroad had come through, Charles K. Landis founded Vineland in an attempt to form a model community. Landis envisioned a fruit growing center, and to some degree he was successful. In a few short years, in 1869, Welch's grape juice was developed here. Then in the 1880s, the first glass vacuum bottle was invented in Vineland. The city became a center for glassmaking and food processing, supporting modern-day firms such as Owens-Illinois and Progresso Foods. Hence Vineland became very important to the railroad, even throughout the PRSL era.

(Opposite page, top) WY-346, a Millville-based job, is working in South Vineland on January 26, 1955. The power today is PRR H-9s #536, working northbound to Newfield with ten cars.

(Opposite page, bottom) Just south of Vineland, in Clayville, a large sand pit provided the PRSL with steady traffic. Another PRR H-9s, #5180, is busy with eleven cars on March 8, 1955; WY-346 is working the sand pit spur on this cold but clear day. These 2-8-0s certainly were put to good use on the PRSL, as the PRR was rapidly dieselizing.

(Below) Two miles further south is Millville, where PRR B-6sb #6399 is seen working job 50-A at the old yard, also on March 8, 1955. With their sloped-back tenders, the B-6sb 0-6-0s provided excellent visability to the rear for the engine crew as they made up trains or worked various industrial sidings. Plenty of steam was still in use in 1955 on the PRSL.

(All – Frank C. Kozempel)

MILLVILLE

The railroad reached from Camden to Millville in 1860 and on to Cape May by 1863. With that came an increase in prosperity that propelled Millville into a major glass container manufacturing center. Eventually evolving into large facilities such as those operated by Wheaton Glass Company or remaining small but important such as Armstrong Cork Company's glass plant, the glass industry produced a large volume of both inbound and outbound business for the railroad. By 1900, Millville was second only to Pittsburgh in volume of glass produced. Throughout the PRSL years, sizable traffic still existed, although in later years most of it had become just inbound raw materials.

(Above and below) On December 5, 1954, a pair of Pennsy H-9s 2-8-0s, #3597 and 5180, await their next assignments at the Millville engine facility. Since 1952, the PRSL relied on the PRR and Reading to supply needed steam power to supplement their own Baldwin diesels.

(Opposite page, top) WY-33 is arriving on February 21, 1964. The power is 6023 and 6022, regular engines on the run during this period. During civic improvement projects in the area in the mid-1950s, the Millville passenger station and freight yard were relocated from the downtown area to a location about one mile to the north. The new yard office, built in 1956, is seen to the right.

(Opposite page, bottom) The 6002 and 6025 idle in the yard on February 26, 1966. The diesels will shortly power WY-34 as it returns to Camden with many cars loaded with sand gathered from surrounding branches as well as some products from the nearby glass plants and other manufacturers.

(This page – Frank C. Kozempel, opposite page, top – John P. Stroup, opposite page, bottom – William M. Tilden)

MANUMUSKIN

Along the old West Jersey and Seashore's Cape May line, the area south of Millville contained many excellent deposits of sand suitable for both industrial and construction purposes. The branch from Manumuskin to Mauricetown however, was built in 1887 to tap the growing market for Delaware Bay oysters. Use of the railroad diminished greatly due to competition from independent truckers in the 1930s and 1940s and a blight in the oyster beds in the 1950s was so great that the industry never fully recovered. The trackage south of Leesburg was removed in 1953 and in 1969 the segment south of Dorchester was abandoned.

(Above and below) About seven miles south of Millville, WY-351 is shown at the G.F. Pettinos sand plant in Manumuskin, as the 6027 works with a good-sized train on April 2, 1968.

(Both – John P. Stroup)

GRENLOCH BRANCH

The former Atlantic City Railroad branch to Grenloch was connected to the Millville Branch at the north end of Gloucester City shortly after the PRSL consolidation. The branch had begun as an independent three-foot gauge line between Kaighn's Point, Camden, and Mt. Ephraim. After the Reading acquired the line, it was standard-gauged in 1885 and extended to Grenloch in 1891. Passenger service continued until 1934, and local freight service continued to several on-line suburban communities. By the early 1970s the largest source of revenue was the industrial park at Bellmawr, often confused with Belmar, a seashore town in northern New Jersey bearing a same-sounding name.

(Above) Train #23-A is passing the Blackwood station with the 6020 as power on June 10, 1971. By this date, this station was the only railroad building still remaining on the line and would soon disappear as in 1973 the four miles below Glendora were abandoned.

(John P. Stroup)

GRENLOCH SECONDARY TRACK

Interlocking	Interlocking Station	Block Station	Block-Limit Station	STATIONS	Dist. from Camden	Sidings Assign. direc'n Car capacity 50 ft. cars		
						North	South	Both
X	X	X		BROWN	2.8			
				MT. EPHRAIM	6.3			
				BELLMAWR	7.4			
				RUNNEMEDE	8.7			
				GLENDORA	9.4			
				BLENHEIM	11.3			
				BLACKWOOD	12.0			
				LAKELAND	13.1			
				GRENLOCH	13.4			

X—indicates in service continuously.

WILLIAMSTOWN BRANCH

WILLIAMSTOWN SECONDARY TRACK

Interlocking	Interlocking Station	Block Station	Block-Limit Station	STATIONS	Dist. from Camden	Sidings Assign. direc'n Car capacity 50 ft. cars		
						North	South	Both
B	B	B		GLASSBORO	18.2			
				DOWNER	22.1			
				ROBANNA	24.0			
				CHURCH STREET	25.2			
				WILLIAMSTOWN	25.7			

B—indicates in service part time.

Leaving the Millville line at Glassboro, the Williamstown Branch was only used occasionally by the mid-1960s. The last railroad building left was the freight house at Williamstown. Built by a Reading predecessor in 1883, the track was abandoned in 1969.

BRIDGETON BRANCH

BRIDGETON SECONDARY TRACK

Interlocking	Interlocking Station	Block Station	Block-Limit Station	STATIONS	Dist. from Camden	Sidings Assign. direc'n Car capacity 50 ft. cars		
						North	South	Both
B	B	B		GLASSBORO	18.2			
				AURA	20.6			
				MONROEVILLE	23.7			
				ELMER	26.3			29
				PALATINE	29.2			
				HUSTED	31.0			
				FINLEY	34.5			
			X	COHAN	36.4			
				IRVING AVENUE	37.7			
				COMMERCE STREET	38.2			
				BRIDGETON	38.9			

X—indicates in service continuously.
B—indicates in service part time.

The Bridgeton Branch also diverged at Glassboro and survived longer, due in no small part to its link to the Cumberland County seat.

Reached by rail in 1861, Bridgeton was home to many manufacturing firms, including several glass container companies dating back to the 1830s. In later years it also became known for its food processing, with firms such as Hunt-Wesson and P.J. Ritter. In nearby Deerfield, Seabrook Farms and Birdseye Products were pioneers in frozen food development.

PRSL passenger service on this rural line ended in 1952. With the coming of Conrail in 1976, the former Pennsy line was abandoned in favor of the Jersey Central route, which was longer but served more customers.

(Above) In typical fan trip weather, an N.R.H.S. trip with RDC M403 is shown at the Bridgeton station on April 8, 1962. In 1961 the Lehigh Valley Chapter covered the Cape May County lines to the Jersey shore and this 1962 trip ran to Deepwater Point and Bridgeton.

(Below) Shown is the Elmer station, mid-way along the Bridgeton Branch, on February 17, 1964. Elmer was a gathering point for agricultural products from the surrounding area and at one time provided the PRSL with a sizable carload business.

(Both – John P. Stroup)

SALEM BRANCH

At Woodbury, the Salem and Penns Grove Branches leave the Millville Branch and strike out to the southwest

(Above) Train WY-51 is shown at this junction, entering the Salem Branch. The power on this August 1959 day is PRR BS-12as #8975, the only unit in its class, taking a day off from its regular assignment to the Pennsy's Pemberton Branch. Since it possessed a steam generator, it was used there in passenger as well as local freight service. Built in April 1951, this locomotive happened to be the first model RS-12 that Baldwin turned out, as it was in the process of upgrading its diesel line. The only major difference between this model and its predecessor (DRS 4-4-1000) was the additional 200 hp. Later Pennsy units of this model came with MU, and two of those had steam generators. #8105 through 8109 were class BS-12am and 8110 and 8776 were BS-12ams. Thus, 8975 remained "in a class by itself." Total Baldwin production of the RS-12 was only 50 units.

Originally assigned to the Lake Region at Cleveland, Ohio, 8975 migrated eastward in late 1957 with BS-10as units 9276 and 9277 from Chicago to become passenger power for the recently dieselized Pemberton Branch. They soon became the backbone of all service on the line, including local freight train CB-20. In preparation for the upcoming Penn Central merger, 8975 was renumbered to 8084 in late 1966, eventually becoming 8306 just prior to the Conrail takeover.

(William J. Coxey)

SALEM SECONDARY TRACK

Interlocking	Interlocking Station	Block Station	Block-Limit Station	STATIONS	Dist. from Camden	Sidings Assign. direc'n Car capacity 50 ft. cars North	South	Both
B	B	B		WOODBURY	8.8			
				PARKVILLE	11.4			
				MOUNT ROYAL	12.7			
				CLARKSBORO	13.7			8
				MICKLETON	14.8			
				WOLFERT	15.9			
				TOMLIN	16.6			
				RULON ROAD	18.6			
				SWEDESBORO	19.5			31
			X	WOODSTOWN	26.4			15
				SOUTH WOODSTOWN	27.1			
				FENWICK	28.6			
				RIDDLETON	30.7			
				ALLOWAY JUNCTION	32.1			
				PENTON	33.7			
			X	SALEM	37.5			

X—indicates in service continuously.
B—indicates in service part time.

SWEDESBORO

First reached by rail in 1869 from Woodbury, Swedesboro developed into a center for canning and packing of various agricultural products.

(Above) Having traversed over ten miles of rural and agricultural lands from Woodbury, WY-51 eases past the station at Swedesboro on February 17, 1964, enroute to Salem behind the 6001.

(Below) In April 1973 a southbound Sunday extra, with #2007 leading, rolls south of Swedesboro. The surrounding fields will soon be green with crops, as acre after acre is under contract to Campbell Soup Company and others. Along the farmland branches during the summer, the trains could be seen stopping occasionally as the crews would gather a grocery bag full of tomatoes thanks to a friendly farmer.

(Above – John P. Stroup, below – William J. Coxey)

WOODSTOWN

SALEM

(Above) Seven miles further south, at Woodstown, a fan trip is shown with RDC M405 on May 26, 1963. This is the third of four annual trips sponsored by the Lehigh Valley Chapter of the N.R.H.S., which together covered the entire PRSL. This one also went to Millville and Leesburg. The 1964 trip traveled to Atlantic City, Mays Landing and Somers Point. The last regular passenger service to Salem ended in 1950.

(Below) PRR 9328, a leased GS-4 (GE 44-ton) sits beside the frame Salem freight house, also on May 26, 1963. Less than a month afterward, on June 21, another PRR unit, Baldwin switcher #9000, was destroyed here by fire that also consumed the rear of the freight house. Pennsy retired #9000 from the roster on May 6, 1964.

(Both – John P. Stroup)

About eleven miles south of Woodstown the railroad reaches Salem, having continued its passage through some of the richest farmland in the state. Salem, the county seat, was first served by rail from Elmer (on the Bridgeton Branch) in 1863. The surviving line into Salem was via Swedesboro, completed in 1883. Salem grew into a major center for glass container manufacturing, hosting the plants of Wheaton and Anchor Glass. Surrounded by immensely productive farmland, Salem also became home to numerous packing and canning companies. By 1900 there were thirty canneries in Salem County, with the H. J. Heinz Company establishing a major plant in Salem in 1906.

PENNS GROVE BRANCH

Laid down in 1876, the line to Penns Grove would prove to be by far the PRSL's most profitable branch. Leaving the Millville Branch at Woodbury, the branch parallels the Delaware River. Unlike the lines to the east however, this route is not so agriculturally oriented, but instead hosts major industrial complexes. One such venture is the Deepwater Generating Station of the Atlantic City Electric Company. The line was extended to Deepwater Point in 1928 in anticipation of the 1930 opening of the power plant. Although located on the riverfront, the utility in later years has received all of its coal by rail.

(Above) One such coal movement is shown passing Woodbury early on January 16, 1967, powered by PRR 1403-3551-2205-7251, a mixture of EMD diesel models (F7a-F7b-GP30-GP9).

(Below) A short while later the cabin car PRR #477575, is rolling through Thorofare, having just passed under the Route 130 overpass. The Focal orange color sharply contrasts with the new Chevy parked nearby.

Once the train arrives at the power plant, the Atlantic City Electric Company will employ their two orange GE 4-wheel switchers lettered "Deepwater Operating Company" to spot the cars for unloading.

(Both – John P. Stroup)

(Above) En route to Pavonia utilizing borrowed Reading RS-3s #471 and 491, WY-842 is seen at Paulsboro exactly one year later, January 16, 1968. This train was scheduled to connect with Pennsy's Pavonia to Conway (Pittsburgh) train PW-1 primarily to expedite DuPont traffic from Carney's Point. By this time, the RS-3s were becoming less favored on the Reading, which was continuing its purchases of second-generation power, including the EMD SW-1500. Therefore, if the PRSL needed a pair of RS-3s occasionally, the Reading could easily provide them.

(John P. Stroup)

PENNS GROVE BRANCH AND DEEP WATER POINT SECONDARY TRACK

Interlocking	Interlocking Station	Block Station	Block-Limit Station	STATIONS	Dist. from Camden	Sidings Assign. direc'n Car capacity 50 ft. cars		
						North	South	Both
B	B	B		WOODBURY	8.8			
				WEST END	9.7			
				THOROFARE	11.6			
				PAULSBORO MOVABLE BRIDGE	13.7			
			X	PAULSBORO	14.8			47
			X	GIBBSTOWN	17.1			52
				REPAUPO	18.6			
				BRIDGEPORT	20.7			
				BRIDGEPORT MOVABLE BRIDGE	21.3			
				PROSPECT	22.0			
				CENTRE SQUARE	23.4			
				JUMBO MOVABLE BRIDGE	24.0			
				JUMBO	24.2			
			X	PEDRICKTOWN	25.0			34
				OLDMAN	26.1			
				PERKINTOWN	27.1			
				FRIENDSHIP	28.4			
			X	PENNS GROVE	29.1			
				PENNS GROVE SEC.	29.1			
				DEEP WATER POINT TR.	32.7			

X—indicates in service continuously.
B—indicates in service part time.

PAULSBORO

About six miles below Woodbury, some "local color" at Paulsboro is seen on February 17, 1964: *(Above)* the "A-frame" bridge over Mantua Creek just north of the freight house, and *(Below)* the section house just to the south, with the 6028 idling nearby. This site would be the future location of a modern freight office to serve the many heavy industries in the Paulsboro and Gibbstown area. Down the line at Jumbo, a mile north of Pedricktown, another "A-frame" bridge crossed Oldman's Creek. The bridge over Racoon Creek at Bridgeport is a somewhat more modern swing span.

This area along the Delaware River and the New Jersey Turnpike attracted a "who's who" of major industrial corporations over the years. Thorofare became home to Pennwalt and Shell petro-chemical plants while Paulsboro contains several chemical companies in addition to a large Mobil Oil refinery. Gibbstown has a large DuPont plant originally built in 1880, where the commercial development of TNT occurred. Pedricktown is host to Monsanto and B.F. Goodrich chemical plants. Down in Carney's Point is DuPont's huge Chambers Works, originally built in 1890, and a noted major supplier of ammunition during World War I, and an adjoining chemical dye plant started in 1917. These large production facilities added up to a rich flow of both inbound and outbound traffic for the PRSL on this quite profitable branch. Passenger service ended in 1950.

(Both – John P. Stroup)

GIBBSTOWN

CARNEYS POINT

(Above) Three miles south of Paulsboro diesel teams up with steam as the 6001 and PRR H-9s #474 double-head WY-841 south out of Gibbstown on June 28, 1955. As seen from the Crown Point Road overpass, sixty-five of the eighty-five car consist are loads of coal for Deepwater Point. The branch swings away from the Delaware River a bit here as it avoids the low-lying marshes around Bridgeport. Then it's back to the river at Penns Grove, where the industrial nature of the line resumes.

At the end of the Penns Grove Branch, and to the west, lies the DuPont Chambers Works, served by a railroad extension from Penns Grove in 1906. The Reading also served this facility via car float from Pigeon Point, Delaware.

(Below right) Their SW-900 #13 is seen on the PRSL on May 17, 1969. This plant is a huge complex, complete with DuPont's own GE center-cab switchers to serve the maze of trackage. South of Penns Grove, the Deepwater Secondary Track completed the route to the Atlantic City Electric power plant, located just to the south of the twin spans of the Delaware Memorial Bridge that carries highway traffic between New Jersey and Delaware.

(Above – Frank C. Kozempel, below – John P. Stroup)

PENNSYLVANIA RAILROAD
Bordentown Branch and Pemberton Branch

Of interest were the off-line uses of PRSL power. On the Pennsy's Bordentown Branch, a regular assignment came about due to the joint operation of the New York – Atlantic City trains, including the well-known **NELLIE BLY**. PRR GG-1s handled these trains between New York and the state capital. PRSL power took over at Trenton and operated via the Bordentown Branch to Delair, where access to the Bridge Branch was attained. **NELLIE BLY** was the pen name of a reporter (Elizabeth Cochrane Seaman) for the *New York World* newspaper who decided to better the fictional record of Phileas Fogg in Jules Verne's novel **AROUND THE WORLD IN EIGHTY DAYS**. She finished the last segment of her 1899 trip on the Pennsylvania Railroad between Chicago and Jersey City, arriving home in seventy-two days. The Pennsy chose to name an Atlantic City express in her honor and it became the last named train to operate in southern New Jersey.

(Below) This is the eastbound **NELLIE BLY**, #1070, pulled by the newest PRSL passenger unit, #6027, on December 27, 1960. About ten minutes earlier it made its 11:20 a.m. stop at Burlington, and is seen just east of the mill town of Roebling. Here at Kinkora, the Bordentown Branch makes its closest contact with the Delaware River, in the background. In four months the Atlantic City – New York service would end, leaving only the Camden – Trenton local passenger service to operate on this line for an additional two years. The former Camden and Amboy would then be completely freight-only.

(John P. Stroup)

(Above) A frequent occurrence was the usage of PRSL power on the Pemberton Branch trains. A troop train returns through Maple Shade from Fort Dix behind the 6008 and 6009 on March 25, 1962. This fifteen-car train of empty equipment had delivered 267 trainees to Fort Dix as U.S. Army MAIN 468. Six Pullmans were followed by a Pennsy twin-unit diner #4697 and 4698, six more Pullmans and a Southern Railway baggage car, #571. The last troop train to Fort Dix ran in 1966.

(Below) Here's #6008 again, this time spending the weekend at Pemberton, as seen on February 9, 1964. The commuter train had needed a substitute for its usual Pennsy Baldwin road switcher of 1000 or 1200 hp. Usually whenever the substitution occurred, on Sunday night or early Monday morning an engine crew would bring out the regular engine and take back the PRSL unit. The passenger operation to Pemberton would cease in 1969, bringing to a close more than a century of service. *(Both – John P. Stroup)*

Diesel Locomotive Roster

CLASS	ROAD NUMBERS	BUILDER	BUILDER'S MODEL	HORSE-POWER	WEIGHT	SERIAL NUMBERS	BUILT
EF-20a	2000–2004	GM–EMD	GP-38	2000	250,000	33797–33801	12/67
EF-20a	2005–2009	GM–EMD	GP-38	2000	250,000	34752–34756	3/69
BS-15ms	6000–6005	Baldwin	DRS 4-4-1500	1500	339,600	74752–74757	4/50
BS-8	6006	Baldwin	S-8	800	198,600	75253	5/51
BS-16ms	6007–6010	Baldwin	AS-16	1600	339,600	75804–75807	3/53
BS-16ms	6011, 6012	Baldwin	AS-16	1600	339,600	75850, 75851	3/53
BS-16ms	6013–6016	Baldwin	AS-16	1600	339,600	75852–75855	4/53
BS-12	6017–6020	Baldwin	S-12	1200	240,000	75930–75933	6/53
BS-12	6021	Baldwin	S-12	1200	240,000	75934	7/53
BS-16m	6022–6023	Baldwin	AS-16	1600	331,000	75979, 75980	11/53
BS-16ms	6024–6027	Baldwin	AS-16	1600	339,600	75975–75978	11/53
BS-12m	6028–6033	Baldwin	S-12	1200	240,000	76126–76131	4/56

EMD Renumberings:

2000-2004 re# as Conrail 7660-7664; returned to lessor; resold as follows: 7660 to North Louisiana and Gulf #46 in 5/83; 7661 to Speno Rail Services power car #201; 7662-7664 to Bangor and Aroostook #90-92 in 7/83.

2005-2009 re# as Conrail 7665-7669; returned to lessor; resold as follows: 7665, 7666 to Bangor and Aroostook #93 and 94 in 8/84; 7667, 7668 to Eureka Southern #30 & 31 in 2/85; 7669 not resold due to blown engine.

Baldwin Retirements:

2/25/68 – 6002, 6007–6009, 6011, 6012, 6014, 6026
5/8/68 – 6015
5/3/69 – 6004, 6010
5/30/69 – 6005
5/18/70 – 6000
2/17/71 – 6033
12/17/71 – 6022, 6023, 6027
12/14/72 – 6013
1/1/73 – 6003
11/1/73 – 6001
10/27/76 – 6006, 6016-6021, 6024, 6025, 6028-6032

6007, 6009, 6011, 6014, 6026 traded in on 2000-2004
6002, 6004, 6005, 6012, 6015 traded in on 2005-2009

(Above) Newly-painted #6000 reposes at Pavonia Enginehouse on March 8, 1968. Only this unit and the 6009 received the lettering "PRSL." Notice that the original letterboard across the top of the hood was removed, which had contained the spelled-out name of the railroad. The only PRSL units with the bell over the headlight were the BS-15ms 6000 through 6005.

(Right) One-month old 2003 and 2002 are at Bulson Street Yard in Camden on January 7, 1968. The EMD GP-38 would prove to be a huge success both for EMD and the PRSL. It was unfortunate that the railroad was not able to acquire additional units to more efficiently move its growing freight volume.

(Opposite page, top) On the morning of February 10, 1968, (the tenth day of the Penn Central) this is the line-up at the east end of the former PRR Pavonia Enginehouse. All power shown is PRSL, and will shortly head up various runs. On the left, a pair of new GP-38s is seen, and the old reliable Baldwins will still be used for several more years.

(Opposite page, bottom) Not all operable power got the new look, as witness the 6006, still in its original factory finish at Cooper's Point Yard in May 1970. It still retained this appearance until it was retired.

(This page – John P. Stroup, opposite page, top – Joseph J. Grella, opposite page, bottom – Ronald H. Baile)

Cabin Cars

The first three PRSL class N-5 all-steel cabin cars had been West Jersey and Seashore #200 through 202, built in 1917 and 1919. 201 and 202 were retired in 1969. To replace their large fleet of wooden four-wheel class ND hacks, the PRSL signed a contract in March 1949 with the PRR to acquire nineteen new class N-8 cabins for delivery that fall. However, due to PRSL financial constraints, in February 1950 the contract was changed to nineteen used, but renovated N-5 cars. These cabins, #225 through 243, originally built between 1916 and 1929, arrived in spring 1950. The 237 was retired in 1972, and 241 and 242 in 1973. The remainder became Conrail 18906 through 18922 in 1976.

(Top) Shown in its original livery is #227 at Cape May in January 1961.

(Center) #236 is seen at Camden in November 1968, in new paint featuring a stylized logo.

(Bottom) In 1969, Penn Central's Hollidaysburg, PA shops turned out three class N-11e cabins, #250 through 252 for the PRSL. These became Conrail 18559, 18564 and 18565. The final PRSL cabin car, #252, is shown at Berlin on March 27, 1970.

(Top – William J. Coxey, center – Richard S. Short, bottom – John P. Stroup)

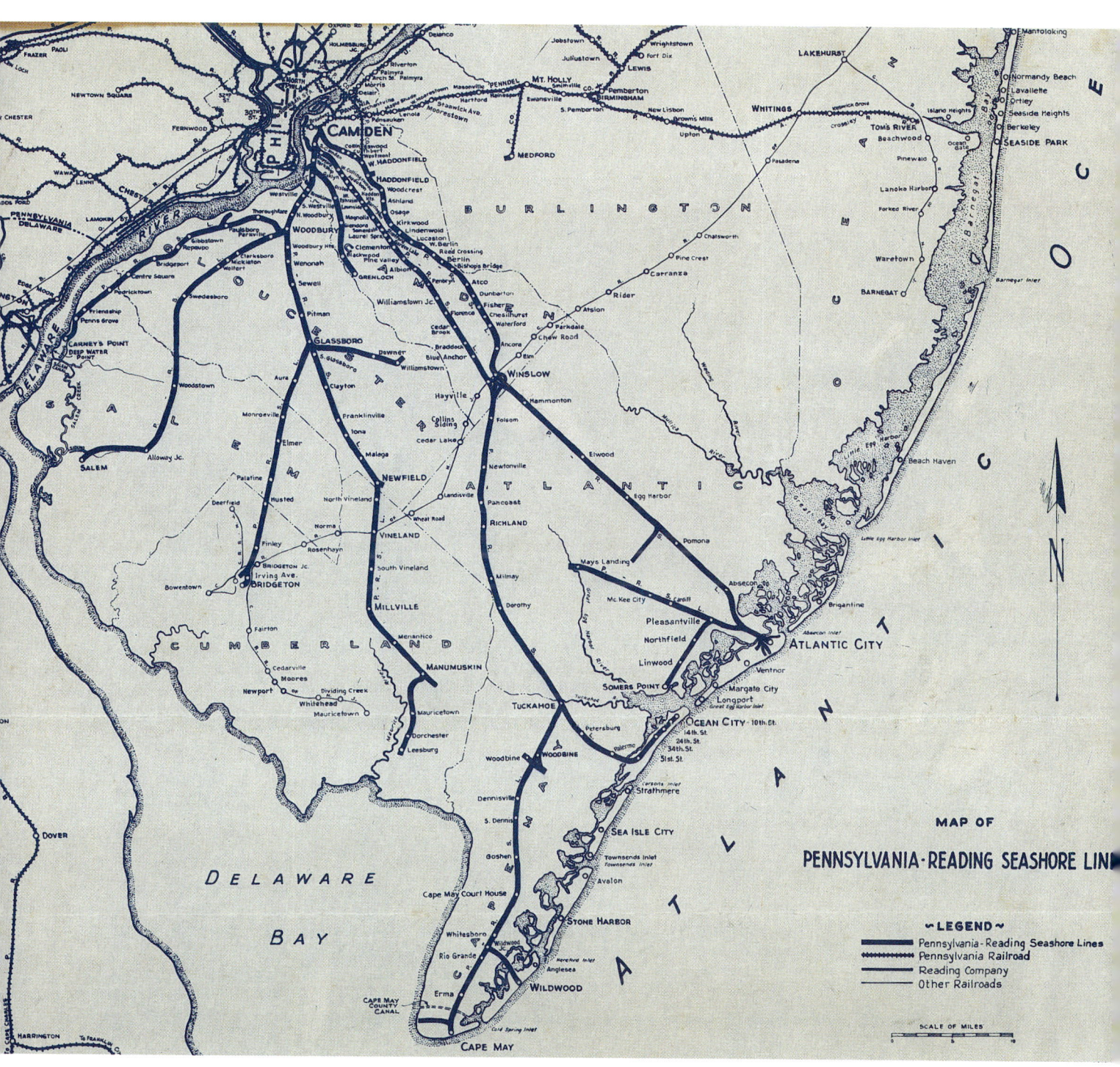

Twilight. That special time when one can reflect on the events of the day. Engines #2002 and 2000 turn at Gibbstown before heading back to Pavonia with train WY-840. At the time of this photo, on November 22, 1969, it was not known that the twilight of the PRSL was so near. After April 1, 1976, Conrail, Amtrak, New Jersey Transit and several short line carriers began to operate most of the former Pennsylvania-Reading Seashore Lines. Although still interesting, that special flavor of southern New Jersey's "own" railroad was gone. Hopefully, it will not be forgotten.

(John P. Stroup)